Who Are We Really?

I0158312

Learning to Listen to Life's Clues

by Robert Munster

TO ORDER ADDITIONAL COPIES OF THIS BOOK, CONTACT:
www.OvertheEdgePublishing.com
or purchase single copies at Amazon.com

Acknowledgments

It is with warm gratitude that I wish to acknowledge Dominque Prevost for his illustrations, Alyssa Monique for the interior design, and Claudia Schwarz for the front cover and author's photos. I am forever grateful to Deborah S. Nelson for her incredible patience and support as my publishing coach.

Dedication

I want to make a special dedication of
this book to all the individuals who were
placed in my life at the proper moment
for my growth and development.
Without their appearance in my life,
this book
would not exist.

Introduction

Throughout my life i have experienced a number of very unusual events. These have happened so many times that i have been unable to deny their existences. In fact, i have come to think of these events as normal, not 'paranormal' or what are considered 'outside' of general human behaviors.

From the age of ten to the present (creeping up on 65), my life has been filled with experiences that defy normal explanations. It has been brought to my attention more than a couple times, that most people do not have such experiences. i find this idea hard to accept. i believe that nearly everyone throughout the world has had at least one experience that has been difficult to explain.

Have you ever seen, or heard the spirit of a relative or stranger and never told anyone about it? How many times have you sensed that something was about to happen and did actually take place? How about dreams that come to pass, or seemingly impossible events that literally saved and/or changed the course of your life?

That's what this book is about. We are constantly told who and what we are from the moment we are able to speak. We are discouraged from talking of 'special friends' or other 'off-the-wall' stuff because people will think that we are weird. In the course of history many individuals were burned, tortured or hung for voicing their experiences or special talents.

The following pages are real-life experiences and events of mine and others whom i have known personally and as a therapist. The time has come for many of us to let go of our fears and speak our truths.

Table of Contents

CHAPTER 1

Early Events

A number of experiences early in my life have had a profound effect on how i viewed events in the following years. i believe these happenings expanded the parameters of what i could accept in the future. Today they seem faintly from another life I lived sometime in the misty past. No matter what i think, they set the tone for what was to come.

My Sister

When i was about seven or eight, one of my younger sisters developed Polio. She was admitted to a special hospital where she had to spend some time in an iron lung tank. i don't remember being allowed to visit her, but played outside by a duck pond while my parents were with her. i do, however, remember walking around the pond worrying whether or not she would die. Somehow i knew that she wouldn't. The ducks and the swans also knew that she would be ok. i don't know how i knew this; i just did.

i believe this experience was one of the reasons i became a therapist as an adult.

The Street Man

At ten years of age, i was sitting in my dad's TV shop on a main street in my town. A man pushing an upright barrel on wheels with an attached broom and dust pan caught my undivided attention. He would take out the broom, sweep the street dirt into the pan, throw the dirt into his

barrel, then off he went to the next corner. The man had a bad limp plus one of his hands was balled up into a fist and curled against his body. It seemed to take every ounce of his energy just to operate the broom and move the barrel.

It didn't make sense to me why this man had to be so crippled and deformed while everyone else seemed so normal. When i asked my dad why this was so, he gave me the strangest look. For that whole summer, every time i saw that street man, i would say, "hi." His voice was very garbled and hard to understand, but i knew that he was saying "hi" back to me. His eyes were so bright whenever he looked at me. He seemed so happy even though walking and talking were difficult for him.

Grampy

Of the six of us kids, i was the only one who spent that summer at my grandparent's house.

My grandfather taught me many things about gardening, fishing and building stuff. He chewed tobacco. i learned very quickly not to spend any time on his right hand side.

It was this summer that he grew very ill and ended up in the hospital dying from heart complications.

At the wake i knelt at the side of his casket. i made the sign of the cross and did all the necessary things i was supposed to do.

When i looked at his face it was obvious that he wasn't there anymore. Then, suddenly, there he was, floating right above his body. He began to tell me that he was fine; in fact, he felt better than he had for years. He said he didn't hurt anymore. He told me to tell everyone that he was ok; that death was not real.

Needless to say, i was a bit shocked. i was petrified and didn't say anything to anyone. I was twelve years old, for God's sake. i told not one soul until i was twenty one.

The Shark

i have always had a healthy fear of sharks, especially since i started surfing. However, nothing had prepared me for the following experience.

At eighteen, i was sitting on a surfboard in the water next to a pier in northern New England. A few of us were in the water waiting for the next set of waves; something we had been doing all summer long. i happened to look down into the water right next to me.

i saw a shark bite my leg off. Startled, i turned around and started climbing up this rope ladder that was hanging over the side of a huge, wooden ship. As i got closer to the top, some pretty gruff looking guys pulled me over the edge and flopped me onto the deck. i noticed that their faces looked worried and concerned. i looked down at my leg. It was ripped off and there was blood everywhere. i knew that i was going to die.

As soon as i realized that i was dying, i popped right back into my body sitting on the surfboard. i was completely disheveled. i paddled in, sat on the beach and wondered whether i had lost it. Nothing like this had ever happened to me before. i had absolutely no idea about past lives or anything close to this except for the experience with my grandfather. Needless to say, my buddies thought i was nuts; maybe a bit too much partying.

Over the next few days, i assumed that the experience was saying something about my abnormal fear of sharks; why i was constantly looking for sharks, even in lakes and swimming pools. It wasn't until a few years later when i began having some past-life recalls, that i understood what had happened that day.

CHAPTER 2

Past Live Recalls

Since my event in the water with the shark, i have experienced a number of past life events. In the beginning i was disturbed by these unexplainable happenings, but after experiencing many of them, they became as natural as any other part of my life. i am only entering a few of them here as many hold information which is too personal to share here.

Sydney, Australia

During my tour in Vietnam, i experienced a number of psychic incidences such as precognition (knowing things before they actually happened). It was a time i explored the concepts of karma and reincarnation. After all, being in Vietnam, i was living in a world of Buddhists. These new ideas became fascinating explorations and mental adventures for me. On a number of occasions i noticed that my own familial, social and religious conditionings did not fit the realities of the environment in Southeast Asia. My mind opened to the possibility of having lived another life before this one. i finally told someone of the experience at my grandfather's funeral. He didn't think i was strange at all; in fact, this guy thought that it was cool.

While on R&R in Sydney, i experienced an enlightening, yet disturbing, event. While staying at a local hotel, i was standing in front of the bathroom mirror preparing to go out when another face showed up in the glass for a brief second. It had my eyes and nose structure, but the rest of the face was very unlike mine.

i wasn't afraid; more curious than anything else. I spoke out loud (i have no idea to whom) saying, "i want to see some of my past lives." Nothing happened so i stated, "i'm not leaving this spot until i do." i remained in front of that mirror for a full 45 minutes. i focused every ounce of my will and attention; i was determined. Finally, the faces came, five of them, four men and one woman. Again, my eyes and nose remained the same, but the whole face, color of hair and amount of facial hair changed. i seemed to know each one of them including something about their lives. This, i thought, was very cool.

Just as i was getting into it they disappeared. i said, again, out loud, "i want to know more, give me more." Suddenly my attention was drawn to the window, where one of the faces appeared in the glass. i heard a voice in my head saying, "If you want more, come join us." Whoa! i grabbed my jacket, bolted out the door, and, unwilling to wait for the elevator, ran down the ten flights of stairs and onto the street. i was scared to death, vowing never to ask for anything like that again.

i was standing on the sidewalk, shaking from it all when i saw my date walking down the street. With her face all lit up, she looked like an angel to me. In fact, her name was Sunny. i was so happy to be alive at that moment.

Sunny had a rare disorder that would require a number of surgeries to remedy. However, she didn't want any of them, no matter what anyone said.

We kept in touch by writing letters regularly. We even talked about getting together when i was out of Vietnam and the military.

About one year later, i was sitting on a hill overlooking a northeastern bay trying to figure out how i could possibly get out of the army. i happened to glance up, and saw a dog crossing the street about 100 yards away. i watched, unable to turn away, while the dog walked directly over to me, laid down and put its head on my lap. No sniffing, no petting, nothing. It looked up into my eyes just as i heard a voice in my head say, "i'm leaving now; i love you." The first thing that popped into my mind was Sunny; she had come to say goodbye. Immediately the animal stood up, looked right into my eyes again and wandered off the way it had come.

i never heard from Sunny again.

The Queen

Throughout my first marriage i always felt that my wife was 'above my station.' She grew up in a very different socio-economic class than i did. i believed that was the reason i felt her to be better, or wiser, or more powerful than i could ever be.

At my son's wedding, years after our divorce, i felt uncomfortable being in her presence. At one point i said to my date, "i need to get out of here. Let's go for a walk."

The B&B people told us about a nice little hike in the woods about two minutes away, so off we went.

Approximately five minutes down the trail, my date put her hand on the back of my shoulder. Wham! Suddenly there was a sword sticking through my shoulder from front to back. Holding the hilt was a queen, my ex-wife. She was twisting the sword while the king, behind her, was urging her on. Instantly i became aware that i had been her court lover. However, I refused to give her that pure, heart and soul kind of love that i shared with another woman (a servant in the castle). If she couldn't have that from me, then no one would. She killed me. i immediately popped back into my body in the present time. i then realized that the queen no longer had any power over me, then or now.

When we returned to the festivities, i gazed right into my ex's eyes. We both knew that the power gig was finished. i wasn't certain that she consciously "got it, "but it was clear that somewhere inside of her she knew something had changed. i felt a sense of freedom. Since that experience, it has been easier to communicate with her.

Another Life Ex-Wife

When i first met Dee (not her real name), i felt a strong attraction to her as if i knew her from somewhere. She felt something also, yet, the very next day pushed me away vehemently. After a few years of working together in therapy programs, we finally came to a truce and

began to form a deepening friendship. On occasion we traded treatment sessions.

It was my time on the table. With her help, i was able to release asbestos from my body that i had picked up from the pipes in the basement of my elementary school. i could see the coating on the pipes and feel the glass-like fibers entering my bloodstream and exiting into my bladder. That was totally amazing all by itself.

However, once that was finished, the scene completely changed. i was lying on a roughly hewn, kitchen table looking up at a thatched roof inside a small cabin-like house. It was dark, wet and cold inside the walls made of sod.

i was badly injured from a battle. My clothing seemed to be of the middle ages. i noticed this woman standing over me; it was my friend, Dee. She was, at that time, my wife. She was crying because i was dying. We were having a fight. She and her father wanted me to have a religious ceremony (a formal funeral or something similar) and i wanted nothing of the sort.

As i died, i told her i was sorry that i had to leave her. i also told her that i loved her very much. Then i died. Next thing i knew i was back on the treatment table with her above me, tears pouring down her face. We held each other for a few moments, both understanding that this experience explained our personal history this lifetime. We both remarked on feeling a sense of completion and freedom from our past. Since that time there exists a strong understanding between us.

Political Death

During most of this lifetime, i have felt that i would be killed if i were to speak of political wrongdoings or of crimes against humanity. This sense of doom has been quite strong at times, especially when i consider publishing anything which opposes the political or economic powers that be. A few years ago, i contracted the flu, along with a high temperature and fever. Bed-ridden, i dreamt extensively during two entire days. One of the dreams was about living in Paris. It was one of those Technicolor dreams with colors, sounds, smells – as vivid as being awake.

As a political leader, one of my personal goals for my countrymen was human rights. This was not popular among the current political leaders of the times. i had grown ill and was hospitalized. The beds were the 'old style' with bars on the rails. My wife was close by. Thinking i was asleep, or comatose, she was carrying on a conversation with a man in the room. They were talking about how the poison worked and what would happen now that i was 'out of the way.' While lying there, i realized that my own wife had been poisoning me for months to prevent me from interfering with the status quo of the government.

When i returned to the present day, i understood how the dream related to my present day relationship. It is Interesting how most of life's experiences and lessons boil down to the conflict between love and power.

CHAPTER 3

Animals

People are funny when it comes to the subject of talking or listening to animals. Many emphatically reject the idea that animals, or mammals, can communicate with humans. They are convinced that we cannot understand them or vice versa; animals can't understand what we are saying to them. Yet, at the same time, most people know when their dog or cat is hungry or needs to go outdoors to relieve themselves. How is this possible then, that an animal can communicate these things with just a look in their eyes or on their faces? i believe this is changing. Presently, there is an increased acceptance of inter-species communication. TV shows like Lassie and Rin-Tin-Tin made a believer out of me at an early age.

A vague memory of mine is somewhere around eight to ten years of age when my family lived out in the middle of the woods in northern Maine. i mean, literally, out in the woods - very few houses - more critters than people – we couldn't see the closest neighbor's house/cabin. While wandering through the forest one day, i came upon a raccoon too weak to walk. i went to our house for a box. When i returned "the guy" was right where i left him. Thinking nothing of it, i picked him up, put him in the box and took him home. i fed him every day for two or three days before he died.

My mother was amazed that this wild creature allowed me to handle it. Also a bit freaked out about the possibility of him having rabies, she consistently reminded me to be careful. Since that time, i have felt a special connection to most kinds of animals. Each and every close encounter with them left me feeling amazed that they allowed me to get so close.

Following, are a number of experiences that have unfolded with regards to animals.

Angel

After separating from my first wife, i wanted a dog. i took my two children with me to the animal shelter. The three of us noticed a really skinny Irish Setter who was cowering in the back of its pen. We took her out for a short walk. She trembled so badly that all we wanted to do was calm her down. That was the deciding point; we were hooked. Once in the car, my daughter came up with the name, Angel. My son and i agreed; Angel it was.

The three of us loved that dog as hard as we could. When the kids came for regular visits, they lavished her with love and affection all day long. After about five or six months, she began to fill out into one of the most stunning Setters i have ever seen. Her head and tail came up, her chest out and proud and her feathers flying. All it took was love. People constantly remarked how beautiful and mellow she was, especially for an Irish Setter.

Angel possessed the special ability of getting out of things, like fences, cars, tie downs, etc. Every time i left her at home in the fenced-in backyard, she would be out

on the front lawn awaiting my return. The fence gate, even when secured with a rope, would be wide open, the knots untied and the latch unsecured. The kids began calling her the 'magic dog'. Once we parked approximately a half mile away from a park where fireworks were to be displayed. i left the windows cracked about one inch down, the doors locked with her water dish on the floor. The kids and i found a place to set up right next to a large pine tree. Two minutes later, Angel came strolling right up to us and sat down. The park attendant allowed her to stay with us for the show. Once back at the car, we noticed that the passenger side door was slightly ajar, yet all the other doors remained locked. Had she figured how to open the door? We never found out.

The four of us spent that summer together, completely inseparable. i believe that Angel showed up in our lives to help us through the separation. She was the glue that held us together. We went everywhere and did everything together. In what could have been a very tumultuous time, Angel gave us joy and hope that everything would be OK.

Over the next three years, Angel and i grew extremely close. i was 'in love' with another species. We had such a deep emotional bond and respect for one another which nothing could disturb. We helped each other heal from the wounds of our lives.

There came a time when i had to place her in a kennel while i traveled across the country for a week. Since finding her in the shelter, i had never left her. The owner, a vet, noted my concern and promised that he would pay special attention to her.

When i returned to the kennel, the vet met me at the door. He told me that Angel had died while i was away. He said that she went to the corner of the kennel's cage and watched me as i drove off. She stayed there refusing to move or eat or respond to any of the staff. After three days her stomach began to bloat. He performed surgery on her but to no avail. He said, "She just seemed to give up; she died from a broken heart." He never witnessed a dog do that before.

That was all i heard. To this day, i do not know how i drove the 45 minutes to my house or what happened over the next few days. The next thing i knew, i was at my parent's home one hundred miles away where i spent a few days moping around their home.

Many of us have felt the pain of losing the family pet. It is never easy. They become like a family member and when they die, it is traumatic. In the process of training and bonding with a different species (cat, dog, bird, or whatever animal), a certain amount of behavioral communication must always be present. We ARE communicating with another species of being.

Ralph

We had an hour to kill before the meeting, so i took my dog, Ralph, to a park for some exercise. A couple of minutes into the walk, he took off in the direction of some other dogs. This was a bit strange for Ralph rarely left my side.

As he sauntered over towards these dogs, i noticed that six or seven other dogs began to converge on the same spot. In a matter of moments all the dogs (about ten in total) formed a circle around Ralph. From the center Ralph turned to face each dog one after the other. He spent a brief time looking directly at each one as though he was telling that particular dog something that was meant for only him/her. As soon as he finished with them, they all broke away, returning to their respective owners. Ralph came straight to my side. He told me that we could go now.

Each person involved stared at this event in complete amazement at what transpired. Some walked away simply shaking their heads. What on earth just happened here, i thought? Did Ralph actually hold a little Satsang, or discussion, with these other beings or was it just our imagination?

Ralph was an unusual companion. As with most of my dogs, i found him at a shelter. Of the twenty or so to choose from, he made it clear to me that i was to take him home.

As with Angel, he was never more than six feet from my side unless we were in the woods. Even then, he always knew where i was.

i made it a habit to practice 'mental telepathy' with Ralph. He would be lying on the floor seemingly asleep when i would say inside my head, "Ralph, get up and come sit next to me." Within ten seconds he was sitting by my side looking into my eyes asking me what i wanted.

People always loved to be around Ralph. It was difficult for me to leave him at a kennel after what happened with Angel. Perchance i found a kennel about twenty miles from my house. i went there for an interview; Ralph, myself and the owner. She fell in love with him immediately and, him with her. For the first time, he didn't mind my leaving him - he just went right in and snuggled up against her. She greeted him and then led him into his pen. At one point later she told me that he joined her on her rounds of the other dogs. She said that he could calm the nervous ones down simply by looking at them.

About a year later, i returned from a trip. Ralph was out of his pen, right at her side, following her while she did her rounds. i noticed that she didn't look well so i asked if she was alright. She immediately began sobbing as she told me of her bout with cancer including some pretty rough chemo sessions. She said that Ralph's presence helped her make it through this tough time.

She didn't know how or why, but somehow he was able to make her feel better just by being there with her. One look from Ralph's eyes and i understood what was happening.

Ralph was with me for just over ten years. The telepathy between us grew to a point where i could hear him in my head, if not in words, then in images. i can't speak for him, however, it seemed he could pick up my thoughts. He would do the things i was thinking of before i verbalized them. We were way beyond simple commands or needs.

As he grew older he began slowing down. At one point, he began vomiting this horrible looking orange and yellow bile. A few people told me that his end was near. i asked Ralph, "Are you going to die soon?" He told me, "No, not now." i let him know that i would take care of him as long as he needed, no matter what that meant.

About three years later, i was preparing to drive to Florida for the wedding of a daughter of a close friend. Ralph put his head on my lap. He told me that he wanted to go with me; would i please take him on one more trip? At that time he couldn't jump up into the cab of the truck or the back of the camper anymore; i had to lift him. Of course i would take him.

It was hot. We took a break in Savannah. i made a phone call while sitting in a parking lot. Once i hung up, Ralph said to me, "i want a haircut." So, off we went to find a groomer. He was so weak and tired he could barely sit up for the cut. Even though he appeared much cooler without the hair, he was having a difficult time walking.

About one hour from our destination he wanted to stop for the bathroom. i had to lift him down from the cab of the truck. Standing by the side of the highway trying to pee, he started shaking and fell over. i picked him up and put him back in the cab, but he couldn't hold himself up in a sitting position. He looked me right in the eyes. i heard him say, "i don't know what is happening to me; I'm scared. i don't want to leave you. i love you so much."

i held it together long enough to find a vet. When i stood in front of the secretary, i started sobbing, saying that i thought my dog needed to be put down. She led me to a treatment room. i described his symptoms while we waited for the vet to come in. The vet listened to my story, and said that he needed to do a test. Right then Ralph had a full- blown seizure. The doc confirmed my thoughts. He left to prepare the solution. As he put the needle and solution in, i held Ralph's head in my hands, telling him out loud that he didn't have to come back in another dog's body; i would see him when i left this world. "i love you." Then he slid away. When i looked up, all three of us were crying.

Looking back on my time with Ralph, that pain returns, but it cannot compete with the amazing adventures we shared. If i had not taken the time and patience to

explore our communication, would it have been the same? How deeply can we connect with those other species in our immediate environment?

How much richer do our lives become when we listen to our pets?

A Helpful Horse

For as long as i can remember, i have feared horses. However, every now and then, one enters my life in a special way. When separating from my children's mother, my supervisor graciously invited me to stay at her home with her family until i could get my bearings.

In back of their house, they kept a horse. Nightly, i went down to the small paddock to spend time with the horse and play my flute. The melody flowing out of me was terribly sad, of course. The mare would come close and stare at me while i lamented through my music.

Well, one night, she came really close. She looked deep into my eyes like she wanted to tell me something. Immediately i heard a voice in my head saying, "Open the gate and climb on my back." Without the tiniest amount of fear, i thought, "Don't i need a saddle?" "No," she said, "i will show you how."

For twenty minutes or so, she carried me along a pathway. In the matter of a few moments, i knew exactly what to do in order to maintain my seat on her back,

even when she ran. Every so often i heard her voice telling me that she could take some of my pain.

Back at the paddock, we touched our heads together. i thanked her profusely for her help. She told me that she really enjoyed my flute playing. She also said, "Eventually it will be alright; the pain will go away. It has been my pleasure to assist you with your burden." The lines of differing species fell away. We were two souls, one helping another. This time it was my turn for help.

Schooled by a Bear

People expect unique experiences with tamed animals and pets. They are quite common and easily accepted by most people. Not so with wild creatures. In a natural environment, things can be very different and, sometimes, dangerous. It is much more common for people to fear wild critters. i am no exception.

Fishing on a small stream, just outside of Hyder, Alaska, i hooked a 30lb salmon on my fly rod. Hooked well, and working it, keeping the tip up with the line taut, i played the fish like i knew what i was doing. Suddenly a good-sized black bear popped from out of the dense brush on the opposite side of the stream. *Holy shit,* i thought.

i began letting out line and back-stepping towards the truck, ready to drop everything and bolt for the truck and my life. Watching the bear intently, i noticed it look at the fish flopping in the water, then back at me, then back at the fish. He seemed puzzled at this odd creature and his peculiar behavior. In one fell swoop he dipped his head into the stream coming up with a huge salmon drooping from both sides of his mouth. He looked directly into my eyes; and i heard the following words in my head. "This is how you do it, stupid." Then he disappeared back into the bush.

My knees shaky and weak, all i could do was laugh. i released the fish and left the area knowing that i had just received my first fishing lesson from a true local.

A White-Tail Deer

Almost every hunter knows how skittish white-tail deer can be. Once they get your scent, they high-tail it out of the area. i believed this also until i had the following encounter. We were driving north on a dirt road somewhere on the western side of Glacier National Park, Montana. i passed a rather large meadow when i noticed four of them gathered around a depression in the ground. Something inside me said "stop!"

Grabbing my camera, i jumped out of the truck and started slowly walking towards them. Immediately, three of them bolted – no surprise. One, however, the biggest of all (a healthy, Western four- point buck) stayed at the hole. i approached cautiously while continuously speaking in a soft voice, telling him that it was ok. "i'm just going to take a few pictures. This is the shutter that you hear." i moved to a large rock about twenty feet

away from him. i sat and watched, all the time talking softly to him. i was astonished that he allowed me to stay so close. He scratched at the gravel hole until water filled the small depression. Then he lowered his head to drink, always keeping an eye on me. When the water was gone, he did it again.

Suddenly he went stiff, head up, on full alert. He bolted to the edge of the clearing where he stood, stock still, tail high in the air, just watching. i popped off some amazing photos where i could actually denote the muscular ripples in his thorax. He was 'at the ready' for three or four minutes before walking back toward the water hole.

For a reason unbeknownst to me, i set my camera down and entered the depression. Getting down on my hands and knees, i began to scratch at the hole with a rock. Lo and behold; up came some water. i put my head down while making lapping and slurping sounds as if i were drinking from the puddle. He stood there watching me.

When i stopped and stood up, he trotted about eighty yards up a small incline in the meadow. i followed him. When i approached to within fifteen or twenty feet from him, i noticed that he was urinating. Not wanting to seem like an alien, once he finished, i did the same. He watched and seemed to understand exactly what i was doing. From the way he looked at me, it made sense to him. As if on command, we both began to walk side by side (about eight feet apart) back to the watering hole.

My wife filmed almost the entire event. She was completely amazed at what she witnessed. We climbed back into the truck leaving the meadow as the buck watched us drive away. For the next hour i felt a strong sense of honor and gratitude for this remarkable time that i shared with a wild animal which is typically weary of humans.

Now, don't get me wrong. i am not advocating walking up to any wild animal that you encounter. If you feel any sense of fear or danger, don't try anything foolish.

However, there are situations that present themselves which can afford us an extraordinary experience with another species.

The Consoling Chickens

We never know when, or from where, we will receive little lifts to help us through trying times. Whether we are ready for them or not, these assists can come from the strangest of places or from the most unlikely creatures.

i built a chicken tractor for some Rock Cornish hens i was raising. Each day i pulled the wheeled coop to a different spot in the yard where they could graze on fresh grass and bugs. Plus, they fertilized the lawn – what a deal. Every time i fed them, or moved the tractor, i talked to them.

They never really seemed to pay much attention to my yacking away; they just wanted the food. Or so, i thought.

One day was emotionally heavy for me as i hauled the contraption to new turf. Never the less, i kept right on talking while i changed their water and feed. Upon finishing the task i sat down on a nearby chair and cried. A moment later i noted a new sound that i had never heard from the chickens before. It was like a cooing, both mellow and soothing at the same time. i looked up to see that all eleven birds had left their food, moved to the edge of the pen and stared at me. Instantly i knew that they heard my pain. They were telling me that they, too, knew of suffering. i felt so much better. i thanked them and wandered off to the next chore in much better spirits.

Do all creatures share similar experiences? i was beginning to believe that they do. We simply don't pay attention.

CHAPTER 4

Dolphins

My experiences with dolphins are numerous and memorable. These events have touched me so deeply that i am certain to shed tears of joy and gratitude as i write of the following accounts. Since the age of four, swimming like a dolphin has been a natural form of movement for me in the water. Having been a surfer from the age of sixteen, i have been fairly close to a number of them. Sailing in some of the world's oceans, one can't help but encounter these curious and playful beings. So, when the opportunity came for me to be in the water with them, i was beside myself with excitement. For two months prior to my first close encounter, i read everything i could find. i learned about dolphin anatomy and all of the 'do's and don'ts' of dolphin etiquette.

The day finally came. The twenty minute boat ride to the lagoon took three or four forevers. Off the boat and up the ramp we went--twelve therapists ready for our first dolphin swim. There they were, jumping and flipping; i thought i would literally burst apart from the excitement of it all.

We were split into two groups of six; i was in the second group. Charged with excitement, i couldn't sit still. i asked if it was alright for me to put my feet in the water over the edge of the platform. As soon as my leg entered the water, one of the dolphins swam by scraping its lateral fin against my leg. i heard perfect English in my head saying, *What are you waiting for? Come on, let's play?*

My immediate response was, *i can't, it's not my turn.* i felt like a six year old.

Finally it was my turn. Immediately a dolphin was at my side. We swam and dove and spun around, all the while touching or very close to one another. After fifteen minutes or so, i was exhausted. i telepathically let him know that i needed a breather. Instantly, he was gone only to return five minutes later for more. i was as high as a kite. i knew that i would never be the same again.

Two days later we returned. This time our assignment was to act like clients whom we supported in the water while the dolphins did what they did. To look into their eyes could be considered an invitation to play which is a no-no in therapist etiquette. Our 'mission' was to direct the attention of the dolphin to the client whom we were holding supine in chest deep water on a platform.

i was holding my therapist/client when one of the dolphins stopped right in front of me. i could feel her eyes boring into my brain, wanting my attention. i held fast to my task when she came right up beside me and began persistently raking her lateral fin against my leg. i finally said inside my head, *What do you want?* Again, in perfect English, i heard, *i need you to move her (the client) to the side because I'm going to lift her up. OK*, i said, as i turned her. Sure enough, under the client she went and lifted her up, holding her aloft for sixty seconds or so.

A few moments later she came back to my side rubbing my leg with her lateral fin again. i said inside, *OK, i know. No,* i heard. *This time i am going to lift her head.* She did exactly that. By now i was convinced that something extraordinary was happening.

It was my turn to lie back in the water. i had no idea what to expect when one dolphin began bumping her rostrum (nose) against my left forearm and making a bunch of clicking sounds. i was wondering what on earth that was all about when i suddenly remembered that i fractured that forearm in two places at the age of ten. *Oh my God,* i realized that she was repairing the bones with sound and energy.

OK, enough is enough, i said mentally. *If you are so aware, how about fixing that place between my shoulder blades that no one seems to be able to remedy?* i went on and on for about five minutes before realizing how stupid i was acting. *Wham!* A rostrum rammed into that exact spot. *Ok, i'm a believer.*

For a few moments i went very still and quiet. i began thinking that there is so little love in this world and how difficult it is sometimes for me to live here. Instantly i heard, "Yes, we know, but we (meaning them and me) have come here to uplift others and bring more love to this planet. This is our job. We understand. We hear you and feel your pain and loneliness." Joyful tears flooded from my eyes. i was both deeply touched and connected with another species of being.

This whole first experience left me feeling that i was assisting the dolphins instead of the other way around. They were the experts and i was the client. What a gift.

Over the next couple of years, i learned that one of the females had lost a child. This, the facilitators explained, was the reason why this particular dolphin sought out close personal contact - she was looking for love.

During the last day of the therapy program, another extraordinary event took place. i was a supporting therapist during the four day program. As always reminded, we therapists are not to engage the dolphins except for directing their attention towards the client we are holding in the water. Well, this one dolphin (the one who lost a child) kept coming to me and putting her heart in my hand. Each time this happened i directed the energy into the client just like i was instructed to do.

Out of the blue, the client, a non-verbal teenager, got up and walked away. The lead therapist followed the client leaving me standing by myself in the water. Immediately the dolphin came right over to me, again putting her heart into my hand. She told me to put my other hand on the top of her head over her brain and close my eyes. As soon as my hand settled on her head, her whole body began writhing and unwinding. i felt completely melded with her as we went into what i can only describe as 'another world or dimension.'

After an amount of time (about two minutes), i felt it necessary to disengage from her. As soon as i did, here came the client and the lead therapist. i quickly placed the client between myself and the dolphin saying internally, *it is time for her now.*

For the remainder of the day i felt as though i had been given one of the greatest experiences a human could have. A female dolphin chose me, of all people, to share something remarkable. Little did i know that there was more to follow.

Two days later, during a break between programs, i took the opportunity to spend a day with one of the trainers. She took me to the community pen, had me enter the water, and participate in their training. Following this short session, i fed them.

The second pen we visited belonged to the female with whom i had the remarkable experience. The trainer wanted me to spend some time with her alone in her living pen. i jumped into the water and put on my fins and mask. Immediately she grabbed my hand with her dorsal fin dragging me under the water. She pulled me around and around her pen repeating again and again, *This is my world. Welcome to my home.*

This went on for ten to fifteen minutes. Each time i even thought that i might possibly need a breath of air she took me to the surface, then right back down again. i was holding her dorsal fin with my right hand, being dragged

round and round, when she told me to put my other hand on the side of her face. For the next span of time all i remember is staring into her eye as we soared through the water joined in some kind of loving bond.

Then she brought me to the surface right in front of the trainer whose face held a look of amazement. The dolphin waited in a total vertical position while i removed the mask and fins. As soon as i was finished she sidled over to me placing her lateral fins around my sides and held me. My eyes poured tears from a fountain of love and joy. Words cannot adequately express what i felt at that moment.

When i could talk again, i asked the trainer if this dolphin was always this playful and personal. She told me this was the first time she had shown this kind of joyful animation since losing her baby.

How can such an experience be measured? How could i, or anyone else, negate the awareness or emotional nature of another species after an event such as this? i was 'in love' with a female from a different species.

My Sweetie's Turn

Two years later, i had the chance to bring my sweetie to a special program for the significant others of the therapists. This was a great way to share with her what i was experiencing. Trying to simply explain it was not working.

It was our turn to be treated as a couple in the water with two dolphins, one of which was the daughter of my 'special friend.' Before we lay back in the water, she came to me placing her heart in my hand and nestling her rostrum into my chest. i turned to my sweetie, taking her hand and placing it onto the dolphin's heart. We remained like a triangle of lovers for a whole minute or more.

When we dropped onto our backs in the water, she and another dolphin were all over us, banging my head, pushing our heads and bodies together and splashing us. We reported to each other later that we had felt as though we were being sprinkled with fairy, dolphin dust. It was like being blessed. At one point, i heard, or felt, the mother in one of the other pens. She was telling her daughter to do some special kind of thing to us. She did just that. My sweetie finally understood why i would come home after a program in such an elevated state.

i may never know what actually transpired that day, but i know for certain that we were changed somehow. Both of us were deeply moved. We can remember that experience today with vivid clarity.

A Few Thoughts

i believe that my experiences with dolphins intensified my abilities to hear and communicate with other life forms here on earth. Many of us know exactly what our cat or dog are saying to us, and never question it. Why not, then, believe the same with all living things?

CHAPTER 5

Birds

Interesting experiences with birds of all kinds abound in my life. They continually appear, either with messages or awakenings for me. In general, birds operate on a completely separate energy from animals or mammals. Interestingly enough, they show up at just that precise moment when i need their wisdom. During those particular times, i must send out some kind of hidden ether that only birds can detect.

Seagull

Back in my 'hippie days' i lived in a winter apartment on a beach in southern Maine; and loved to take long walks in the afternoons. This was the first year after Vietnam, and i had much to consider and ponder. Sometimes my mind would wander to the edges of reality, while questioning everything about everything.

One cold, partly cloudy afternoon, while strolling down the beach mulling over a thousand things in my head, i looked up. i felt myself lift right up through the clouds when a seagull appeared directly in front of my field of vision. It looked me square in the eyes and said "What are you doing this 'high', man?"

Bam! i slammed back into my body. It took the wisdom of a seagull to remind me to stay focused and keep my feet on the ground. It has always been more natural for me to soar around the skies and the mental world than to stay on the earth. Things are so much slower on the ground than in the air where one can travel at the speed

of thought. However, i inhabit a physical body, and that is part of the package of 'me.' i am dedicated to living as a whole human being. Thank you, Mr. Gull.

Helping Little Ones

Coming around the side of my Utah house to enter the back door, i found a small sparrow lying on the ground. Apparently it had knocked itself out on a glass window. When i picked it up, i couldn't feel its heartbeat. i thought it dead, however i felt warmth emanating from its small body. i held the little guy enclosed in my hands, chanting and pumping energy into it. i kept this up for two to three minutes. i was ready to give up and pronounce it dead when, suddenly i felt a rush of heat flush through my hands. i opened them up and watched as a perceptible aura surrounded the tiny body. He opened his eyes. i could only imagine what he was thinking as he looked at me.

i held my hands wide open for about ninety seconds before he flew over to a fence, maybe ten feet away. He paused there on the fence looking back at me. Then i heard this tiny voice in my head saying, "Thank you." Then he flew off.

At my present home, small birds are constantly flying into the greenhouse and panicking when they can't get out. They cannot discriminate between glass and no glass, so they continue to fly into glass walls until they're exhausted. Most of them can find the door when i 'shoo'

them towards it. Occasionally, i will have to help. i do so by chanting to calm them down, then catching them lightly in my hands and bringing them outside to set them free.

One time i opened my hands, yet the little guy didn't want to leave. It stayed there for a full three minutes just staring at me as though it was perfectly comfortable in the hands of a giant. i finally had to shake my hands before it flew away. By then, of course, tears of joy were streaming down my face; i was grateful simply to have such an experience.

Great Blue Herons

Everyone knows how skittish Great Blue Herons are; how they never let anyone too close before they fly off to a safer distance. i have never heard of, or seen a Great Blue Heron, sitting on any man-made structures.

One morning, i left my old house to walk the hundred yards or so to the new house i was building. Between the two houses is a cabin. Perched on the roof was a Great Blue looking like he was waiting for me. He allowed me to approach within twelve feet of him. Looking directly into my eyes, he told me he approved of my new house and how i was building it. Once i heard what he had to say, he flew off.

About two weeks later i drove around a curve on a dirt road close to the house. Right in the middle of the road

sat two Great Blues. This is such abnormal behavior--first of all, to be on a road away from water and, secondly, to be there as a pair. i got out of the car to approach them. They allowed me within twelve to fifteen feet of them and didn't take to the air. i felt like something very important was about to happen when another vehicle came tearing up the road. In a flash they were gone. To this day i wonder what would have taken place. i was completely amazed at the fact that they let me so close to them. What a treat.

Condors

Returning to San Diego from Santa Cruz, and driving along the northern California coast, i spotted two huge birds feeding on something by the side of the cliff at a turn-out. Out of pure curiosity, i turned around and returned to check them out. i parked the car about thirty feet away, got out and leaned against the hood.

They were a pair of giant condors, another skittish species. i began talking out loud to them asking if it was okay for me to watch for a while. They didn't take off so i assumed all was well with them.

For approximately twenty minutes i watched as they pulled apart and ate the remnants of a dead fox. i couldn't believe my good fortune to witness such grand and rare birds at such close range. i must have some really "good bird karma."

A car drove by, slowed down, and turned around to see what was going on. As soon as they pulled into the turn-out, the birds took to the air with one stroke of their wings. i had never seen such huge wingspans – incredible. Before leaving, one of them hovered in the air about six feet off the ground, no more than ten feet from me. It felt like it was recognizing something in me, because it just stayed there in mid-air for about fifteen seconds looking into my eyes. i said, "thank you for letting me be so close." With a single stroke, it was off.

Resuming my drive southward, i felt blessed. i actually spent twenty minutes close up with some of the rarest birds in North America. How special is that?

Eagles

Much of my adult life was spent traveling many of the back roads and visiting places like Alaska, Montana and the national parks of America. Hundreds of eagles crossed my path on these journeys. On more than one occasion while driving on some dirt road, an eagle has swooped down out of the sky and flown right by the side of my truck. For a few moments, one will match the speed of the truck and stare right at me while i'm cruising along. i have almost run off the road trying to maintain eye contact with them.

Then they are gone and i am thrilled just to see them close up.

Mt Katadin Locals

i had agreed to embark on a three day mountain journey, backpacking around Mt. Katadin with three younger friends. At the time, i was somewhat depressed, having ended a relationship and considering some possibilities for future directions in my life.

On the long, dirt entrance road to the park, three separate crows flew directly in front of my truck. They were flying at eye level. i could look down their backs, almost like i was flying right behind them. Not one, but three, one after another. i had read in the book, *Animal Speak*, by Ted Andrews, that crows are portents of magic. i knew i was in for something special.

i met up with my friends. We put our backpacks together and headed out. After several miles, we arrived at the first camp site situated next to a lake on the back side of the mountain. While my friends were settling in, i was captivated by a white tail deer in the area. i started walking towards it. i took out some of the carrots i had been munching on, offering them to the deer. To my amazement, the critter walked up to me and ate the carrots right out of my hand. Once he figured out the food was gone, he sauntered off. i turned back towards the camp and my friends who were staring at me with eyes wide and mouths agape.

That evening i had a run-in with a grouse, who stood directly in my path, blocking my way to the lake. We held

our respective ground staring at each other until he was finished and finally walked off. i thought it odd that a wild bird would act in such a manner; it didn't make any sense to me. The next morning we met again as i was walking to the lake for the morning water. This time, however, he puffed up all his feathers, looking like he was ready to do battle. In a soft voice, i asked him what he was so serious about. Just then two females darted across the path and into the brush. i said, "Oh, i get it, you're just trying to protect your women." He looked at me as if to say, "You're damn right." He un-puffed himself and strolled proudly away. i chuckled to myself. *Magic?* Maybe not, but it was magical to me.

On the second afternoon we reached our lean-to; our gear wet from the day's rain. My sleep, what little i got, was riddled with dream after dream. The next morning we climbed a grueling route up the mountain side to the plains leading upwards to the peak. i lagged behind not wanting to miss or lose the rising feeling coming up from deep inside of me. At one point i stopped to take in the stupendous views. It all felt so clean and pure. i felt like i was within reach of heaven and a feeling of cleanliness and purity were rising within me. At that moment, i realized that i was alright; everything would be just fine. i had passed through another trying time and into the present like a phoenix.

The crows were right – Magic!

Whether chickens, sparrows or eagles, when a bird gets close or behaves in a strange manner, i pay close attention. i really never know what to expect, but i am always ready for what they have to show me.

CHAPTER 6

Religious and Mystical Events

A number of events happened to me that fall into the categories of either religious, spiritual or mystical-type experiences. Some of these events included big booming voices, impossible to miss, and others are more subtle, but still life-altering. Each and every one of them has dramatically changed the course of my life.

High School and the Priest

As a senior in high school, i was president of the CYO (Catholic Youth Organization), captain of the church basketball team and a lecturer at Sunday Mass. i was the guy who read the epistle from the pulpit. i would read these passages to the people of my Parrish. My mother was so proud of me. If she only had known some of the "other things" i was doing at the time.

i began having questions about the material i was reading to the people. One of the passages was talking about how Christ had said something like, "You too, can sit at the right hand of the Father. " i took this to mean that we, people in general, could also see God.

Moved by this, i went to the priest and asked him outright, "How do i see the Face of God?" He was visibly taken aback by this odd question coming from a seventeen year old kid. He told me that no one can do that. It is impossible. i reminded him of the passage that i had read in church that very morning. He thought for a really long, uncomfortable moment.

Then he told me quite honestly and sincerely, that he had no idea of how to do such a thing.

By the end of the school year, i was through with being a Catholic. i went to church every now and then, especially when my mother wanted to go. i remember escorting her to many a midnight Mass during Christmas or Easter. Later on, when i traveled to other countries, i regularly visited numerous churches.

My Awakening in Vietnam

Sitting under a rock outcropping above the beach in the South China Sea, Vietnam, i struggled with the idea of how i fit into this life and the world in general. i thought, *What was the sense of it all?* Here i was, on the other side of the world from my home, in a war that i certainly didn't believe in. *Who was i and what was the meaning of it?* For the previous six months i studied Zen Buddhism. i read the Bagavaghitta and sat in a lotus position for an hour every night. Still, nothing was making any sense at all.

With these thoughts in mind, i walked out into the ocean, and stood about chest high in the water. All of a sudden, i could not discern my body as being separate from the water, the air or the land. i felt, for the first time in my life, that i was 'one' with everything - that 'i really mattered.' i felt open and elated as though i had found a long awaited grand truth. i also felt a bit spooked.

i left the water not wanting to disappear into the ethers.

Walking from the water and up a hillside, i felt like i floated above the ground. Every now and then i took a few steps backwards to check the sensation and make sure that i wasn't crazy. Next i returned to the overhang, sat down and pondered about what just happened. i just experienced some kind of connection with the elements of the earth. As i closed my eyes, i began to see snippets of my future flash across my mind like scenes from a movie screen.

That experience changed the course of my life forever. i had awakened somehow from a deep sleep and now it was time to "be aware." i considered that event to be a major turning point in my life. i started formulating my own value system as opposed to those of my country, religion, social or economic background. It felt as though i had just become a citizen of the world. Today, some 35 or 40 years later, those vivid previews are materializing in my outer life.

Once we are awake and open, what great things are we capable of? Are there limits to such knowledge and awareness? Do we go on believing the things we are told or do we become part of a larger scheme of life? Those questions can only be answered by each individual in his/her own way.

Shining In the Woods

During the last part of my military existence i was living with the woman who later became my spouse and the mother of my children. Without her, i would not have made it through the insanity of those days. At that time, while adjusting to my return from Vietnam and still in the active military, i fell into a serious depression. For 4 days i went into an intensely dark world where i was very much alone. i couldn't trust anyone, not even this woman.

One afternoon she and i drove into the countryside. We talked at length about the importance of love and spirit on the drive out of the city. i knew that i needed her help and, more importantly, her love, to help me out of this horrible place.

We found a park with a path, parked the car and headed into the woods. A light rain was falling. i asked inside with all my heart, "please help me." Within one minute a soft light began surrounding her. Then i noticed the same glow around me. It seemed to come from both inside and outside of us until it formed a circle some twenty feet around us. To me, it looked like we were living, breathing angels radiating with pure love. We were both aware of this phenomenon. i had the strongest sensation that a spell had been broken. We were both quite disheveled by this experience, so we decided to hop in the car and head back to the city.

Approximately a half mile from our apartment, i spotted a small bird on the side of the road that appeared injured. i pulled over, got out and approached the little, brown wren. i reached down; he allowed me to pick him up and hold him in my hands. He stayed there for a moment or two, content as could be. He looked into my eyes – i heard a voice telling me, *It is alright, it is going to be ok*. It flew to a fence about ten feet away, then turned back to look at me again. i heard the words, *believe, just believe* in my head. And then he flew away.

How does one explain an experience like this to family and friends? Forget about them, how do i explain it to myself? From that point on, i accepted these unbelievable experiences happening to me. Granted, i still didn't tell many people, however, i did begin to believe, solely because they continued to happen.

Peeing on a Tree

Sometimes in my life, i have received guidance from a source inside that comes across very loudly, and at the strangest times. One would think that such wisdom should show up in a more appropriate setting like in a church or from some old wise man with a white beard and gleaming eyes. Not so for me.

Driving back to Santa Monica from spending a week of skiing in the Lake Tahoe area, i really had to pee, so i pulled over and found a tree. i was standing next to a Doug Fir doing my thing when i heard this loud voice

saying, *You're driving back to Los Angeles. You don't even like L.A. It is time for you to go home.*

"What?" i said, "Wait a minute; i'm peeing by this tree and you're telling me to go home? Where is that? Do you mind? Can't i just go pee in the woods?"

The voice simply repeated, *It's time to go home.* This time i knew where home was but it wasn't just the physical location. i was supposed to go to my inner home; time to clean up my act and live from the inside out. By now i knew it was useless to argue with this higher wisdom which knew much better than i did when it came to my growth. It has always been better for me to get out of the way and simply listen to inner guidance. *Doesn't everyone have this stuff going on inside them?*

By the way, i did move physically also; clear across the United States.

Form Vs Essence

It took me about twenty years to stop reacting to religions and their dogma. i could get downright defensive, sometimes, even offensive about it. All of them 'had the truth'; i was going to strip them of their keys to heaven. They weren't going to have the only way to God. i was pretty relentless, until that is, i had the following experience.

One Christmas eve, i took my Lutheran girlfriend to a

Catholic church for midnight mass. The only seats we could find were right up front on the side of the altar. My hair, long and blond, was hanging loosely on my shoulders.

Once the mass started, i found that my attention was lifted towards the vaulted ceiling. i felt my being rise up above the people and soar high into the ceiling. i was being lifted by something inherent in the people of the Parrish. i realized, as clear as day, that it was the essence of the peoples' love for God that was the whole point of religion. No matter what faith it was, each was a form which could hold Divine Love. Each and every person, and their faith, held varying amounts of this essence. Every religion was a form with which to hold the raw form of spiritual flow – it wasn't about the form at all. i had backwards all these years. My long struggle with accepting religious forms and structures was dissolving as i cruised along the high-vaulted arches of the church.

Literally high as a kite, i felt an elbow jam into my side. Instantly i was slammed back into my body sitting in the pew. i opened my eyes. i was looking into the face of a priest who was directly across the altar from me. By the look on his face, he must have been watching me and sensed that something extraordinary was happening. My girlfriend said, "Stop whatever you are doing. You are disrupting that priest." i didn't answer her.

Throughout the remainder of the service, i caught his questioning gaze.

Who knows, maybe something extraordinary happened to him, too.

Universal Pain

i went through a period of about six months where i cried nearly every day, sometimes profusely.

One day while driving from Salt Lake to Flagstaff, the tears became so heavy that i pulled off the side of the road. i closed my eyes and wept. Suddenly i found myself somewhere in India watching a mother weeping as she watched her son dying of hunger. Then i was transported to Africa viewing a child as she witnessed her parents being murdered. The tears were literally pouring like rain from somewhere deep inside me. i felt overwhelmed by what i could only imagine was universal sadness. For what seemed like a long time (maybe 10-15 minutes) i felt waves of the deep sadness and heaviness of life. i became aware of something else stirring underneath. My heart was opening in a way i have never felt before.

It finally passed and i drove on into Flagstaff for my appointment with a very special healer. It felt as though i had been primed for a special treatment session.

Leaving Utah

Driving home after work one afternoon, i passed by a future residential golf course under construction.

This new community was being built directly on top of a wetland area. i heard myself say out loud, "Those jerks, they will never learn. How dare they destroy so much?" Next thing i knew, i was hearing this inner voice saying, *Don't worry about it; you won't be living here for long.* So, of course, i blurted out, "Wait a minute; where am i supposed to go now?" The reply was, *You'll find out.* "Thanks a lot," i said.

OK, guess i needed to move again; i really thought that i would be living in the Salt Lake area for a long time. Utah is filled with such diversity, plus it is easy to get anywhere in the intermountain west by auto or air. *Oh, well.* i knew i needed to listen to inner guidance; it hasn't let me down in the past.

So, where would i want to live? It has to be someplace i really like. Having lived in numerous places within the intermountain west, i began to travel to some of my favorite places. i explored around the Wallowas in eastern Oregon. i spent some time cruising around Idaho, Montana, Washington, Utah, Wyoming and Arizona. i discovered some very nice real estate, however, they were either too expensive and/or too remote. Nothing moved me.

If i were to relocate, there were certain things i wanted. i made a list:
1. At least 10 acres.
2. Within 60 minutes from an international airport.
3. Within 60 minutes from a symphony.

4. Includes some type of water on the property.
5. A livable structure to live in while i build what i was supposed to build.
6. Would provide the right conditions to grow my own food and medicinal plants.
7. Be close to mountains and/or the ocean.
8. All of this for under $80,000.

Next, i broadened my search to include the Internet. i looked at places in the Smokey Mountains and the Blue Ridge areas including the coasts of North and South Carolinas plus Georgia. Nothing fit the bill. i was growing a bit discouraged and disillusioned with the whole thing, yet i knew that i needed to continue.

One afternoon while considering my plight, i received an inner nudge to go inside and simply ask, *Where am i supposed to be for the greatest good of all, including myself?* Shortly, my consciousness was 'in the presence of' a spiritual traveler whom i recognized. We were in some kind of planning room filled with people involved in numerous tasks.

This guide led me over to a sonar-looking glass panel (like that of a screen in a submarine). Together, we drew a diagram of the US, placing little lights in areas of importance. i recognized a few lights in spots i have either been in or searched for over the Internet. But in this one, small and specific corridor just off the coast of Maine, were thousands of lights. i immediately stated that i would 'absolutely NOT' go back to Maine.

i had spent too much time there and i refused to go back.

Now, here i was, asking for and receiving help from a spiritual giant and carrying on like a child having a temper tantrum. Wham! i was catapulted right back into my body sitting on my couch in Utah. i was angry at the thought of moving back to New England, a fact that took me nearly a week to accept.

i finally made it through my ego tantrum and chose to follow the advice and help of my spiritual guide. It took me an entire year to sell my house—that was another story in itself. Then, after a trip to Bolivia and Peru, including the trek to Macchu Picchu, i landed in Maine.

The adventures of finding the new property and building my own home are loaded with hundreds of small miracles and events that would fill a book by themselves. At times i found myself wondering, who is building whom? From that experience, my gratitude for the magic of life has multiplied a hundred fold.

Oh, and by the way, i received more than everything i asked for on this list AND at a lower price.

Some Thoughts

So many of the experiences recorded throughout this book can be considered as 'mystical' events. Where does one draw the line between what is mystical and what is

simply living in a greater state of consciousness? What may seem miraculous to one individual may be commonplace to another. What did the great spiritual and religious figures who visited this world think was mystical or miraculous? Maybe, just maybe, they were like you and i. Possibly, they just learned to listen to life's clues that they found along the way, some coming from inside and others from the world around them.

CHAPTER 7

Plants and Rocks

Animals, dolphins and birds talking – that is no big stretch. But what does one do when plants and minerals begin talking to you? Do you ignore messages from this sector of life or listen to what they have to say? These were my experiences.

A Douglas Fir in Sequoia Park

During the beginning of the nineties, i went camping in Sequoia National Park with my wife, dad and son. i awoke at the crack of dawn one morning and, not wanting to wake the others, i went for a walk. i sat down on a rock next to a gigantic Douglas Fir tree. Looking up, i noticed that the top was swaying in the breeze. i wanted to feel that movement too, so i wrapped my arms as far around the trunk as far as they would stretch. i actually felt it moving with the wind. *That was cool,* i thought. i wondered, *If this tree could talk, what would it have to say? It has been around for such a long time, it must have seen a lot of stuff.* i stilled myself and just listened.

Suddenly images appeared on my mental screen. Scenes emerged when the trees were younger. Images of antique cars, people cutting the trees and storms with lightning flashes began streaming across my mind. After a moment or so, the images came and went so fast, i couldn't keep up with them. i broke my contact with the tree and sat back down on the rock. i was a bit shaken up.

How could a tree send so many images so fast ?

African Violets

In the mid-nineties, i experienced a really rough period in my life. i cried every day for six months. My friends, professional cohorts and family members all thought that i might just go off the deep end and never come back. i, on the other hand, knew that it was extremely important for me to release everything that was coming through me. The only way i knew how to do that was to cry. Some days i shed only a few tears and others, i cried rivers all day long. Other people drink or use drugs to survive, i cried.

One afternoon, i was sitting on my living room couch looking at the mountains. i happened to glance at my collection of African violets on a table in front of the window. They were glowing more than i had ever noticed before. As i gazed at them, their glow increased. i thought, *Hey, you know that i see you glowing.* Their luminance grew even brighter. i began shedding tears of joy in response to their beauty.

At that moment the phone rang. It was my nephew, Shifo. "Hey, Uncle Bob, how ya' doin?" i said, "i'm crying." He asked, "What's wrong?" i told him about my experience with the African violets. He asked, "Have you been smoking dope or something?" "Nope," i said, "i'm going to be alright." Knowing that my behavior is beyond his scope at times, he told me that he loved me and hung up. He didn't quite get it but i understood.

My crying was over. My heart had been opened. i knew that my emotional range had grown over the past six months to encompass feelings ranging from deep despair to that of joy at the mere sight of blossoming African violets. i had become emotionally rich.

i would not wish this painful experience on anyone. However, if an individual can go with the pain and tears as though they are an internal shower, the outcome will be well worth the effort. Since that experience, i have been told by numerous friends and strangers that i seem to have a clean, happy energy around me. Sometimes this is true, sometimes it is not. Whichever, i will take what comes my way.

The Pine and the Sunset

i came out of my sauna for a break. While pouring cold water over my steaming body, i watched the sun sinking into the western treetops. Out of nowhere i heard a sigh as clear as day. Looking around for the source, i didn't see anyone. It was quiet there in the woods – really quiet. i shrugged it off and continued to watch the sunset. Again, i heard another loud sigh. My attention followed the sound to the top of a large Eastern White Pine. The sunshine was brushing over the topmost branches as it was leaving for the day.

A thought entered my mind. *Ah, that feels so good,* the tree seemed to be saying. Grateful for the last moments of sun.

i looked around to see if anyone else had heard this. Wow, i chuckled to myself, *i must be losing it.*

On many occasions since then, i have heard whispering sounds among the tops of trees. i grow frustrated at not being able to understand their language no matter how hard i try. If trees can warn each other of an impending disease, and then automatically develop a resistance to the invading organism, why can't i understand their language?

Carrots

i have come to this point of questioning because of my experience in Sequoia National Park, and carrots – yup, carrots.

My wife loved carrots. She had eaten so many that her skin actually turned orange. Having eaten them for years, she had never planted a seed or raised one, single carrot. Being a gardener, i built her a 3x20 foot raised bed, exclusively for carrots. She planted five rows of seeds, and that was it. She rarely watered them and never, thinned them or aerated the soil around them.

i found this behavior intriguing; that someone would plant seeds and just leave them. However, it was her carrot garden and she was free to do whatever she wanted with it.

About a month later, i walked by the carrot bed and heard a faint voice saying, *We need attention.* i told my woman and forgot about it. i knew they needed weeding and care – they knew i knew. i could sense them crying for help.

One day, as i walked by, i heard all of them cry in unison, *We need help, now!* i couldn't ignore this any longer, so i marched into the house and told her, "come with me; the carrots are calling for help."

We spent two hours thinning, weeding, feeding and fluffing up the soil around them. i encouraged her to talk with them and make certain that they had what they needed in the future.

The very next day when i past by their bed, i could swear they had grown at least two inches during the night. They seemed so happy. That season we harvested some of the best tasting carrots i have ever eaten.

i have always believed that when i put love into caring for plants or animals, that love ends up in my cells once i ingest them. i have made it a habit to bless seeds when i plant, care for and talk with the plants as they grow and thank them when harvesting. That love is never wasted.

i hear so many people arguing and crusading for the lives of animals, but no one ever seems to thank a carrot for giving its life for us.

Two Oak Trees and My House

i had cut down a number of trees in preparation for building my new house. i needed a circular space of approximately sixty feet in diameter to create a round, concrete, floating slab to support the sixteen-sided structure i was about to build. i wanted plenty of space around the edges free from fallen limbs and trees.

With the chainsaw running, i approached a fairly large oak tree i thought should go. Just as i was figuring where to cut the first notch, i heard a voice inside my head say, *Please don't cut me down.* i stepped back, turned off the chainsaw and thought, *here we go again.* i looked at the tree and replied, *How much room do you need?* It clearly said, *About twelve feet.* i pondered this for a moment and decided to move the entire design twenty feet away from the oak. The following day another good-sized oak tree said, *Let me stay. Please don't cut me down.* This one was a little further away from the site, but, what the hell, if it was talking to me, it must be important. i cleaned up the immediate area around the tree and went on my way.

Two years later, a dozen or so of my friends helped me put roof rafters on top of the second floor. We put together a real down-to-earth 'roof-raising' with plenty of food and drink for all. This proved to be a moving experience for all of us. The truck driver was so touched by the love he witnessed that he only charged me half of his normal fees for driving his crane to the building site.

i came down from the roof to take a break. Two of my friends were standing in front of the house with arms folded across their chests and serious looks on their faces. When i asked what was going on, they told me that my house was going to fall down. They showed me how the upright beams started to lean off-center, and if we didn't do something soon, the entire house would collapse in a circular downfall. i told them i couldn't handle that; i needed to get something to eat and drink.

Once i had some food in me and stopped panicking, i walked back to the site ready to listen and act. When i arrived, several people had ropes and come-a-longs tied to the posts at one end and hooked up to the two 'oak trees' on the other. They advised me to tighten the ropes a little bit each day until i was able to secure the roof rafters and keep the house from collapsing.

By saving their lives, the oak trees saved my house. Did they know in advance that this would happen or was it mere co-incidence? Is this interspecies communication real, or just a fluke? i really don't care what it is, it saved my house from falling down. That is enough for me.

Talking Rocks

Two years before i started building my house, my youngest sister, Lizzie, told me of a dream she had one night. She said i built a house with a stone fireplace and two pink rocks in the front. i told her that i was, in no way, ready to build a house and, if i did make a stone

fireplace, i certainly wouldn't put pink rocks in it.

A few years prior to my sister's dream, i was hiking near Escalante, UT. My truck was parked up on the Hogback; i was down in the canyon wandering around. i sat down for a rest and some water when i noticed the most amazing rock on the ground next to me. It had all the elements of the area burned into it from some ancient climatic event. The colors and the textures were beautiful. i remained there for 10-15 minutes, every now and then glancing at, and admiring, this particular rock.

As i stood up to leave, a voice entered my mind, *You have to take me with you.* i immediately replied out loud, "Wait a minute, you're a freaking rock." Again, it repeated itself." Unbelievable," i said, "You are a rock; you can't be talking to me. This is nuts." The thing replied, *You have to take me with you.*

Shaking my head in disbelief, i picked up the stone and commenced the mile walk, up the side of the ridge, to my truck. i didn't give it much of a thought for the remainder of the trip. When i got home, i placed it out in the back yard next to the garden.

Over the next few years, every time i went out driving and roaming throughout the intermountain west (which was often), i ran across rocks that said i had to take them home with me. Sometimes i found more than one, and, some of them were heavy. After five or six times, i gave up reacting and simply took them with me. Upon returning home, i put them out back.

After six months i owned quite an impressive rock/cacti garden that continued to grow until it was time to move to Maine.

Most of my belongings were packed up. i went out into the garden to evaluate whether or not i would take some of the cacti with me. Once there, all the rocks screamed in unison, *You have to take us with you.* i remember thinking, *Holy shit, this is insane.* When back in Maine, a dear friend, Kenny, opened up the back of the moving van and said, "Bob, why on earth do you have these three barrels of rocks (55 gallon drums, mind you)?" i simply replied, "Don't ask."

On one hike up into the hills of Maine, a roundish, large flat rock was adamant about coming with me. It was heavy and i had to traverse some fairly rough terrain to get back. i really didn't want to do it, but i finally succumbed and lugged the sucker back to the truck.

When i bought my new property, i dumped all the rocks in a pile next to a tree thinking that, maybe someday, i will build a new rock garden.

Two years later i had a round floating slab finished and was considering building a fireplace in the middle of the house. i met with a man who had tons of experience with building Russian and Finnish styles of fireboxes. He convinced me to build a round fireplace. He would give me a deal on the special cement and hardware plus allow me to hire his assistant to create it.

He told me that i would need lots of rocks. i thought, *where would i find rocks?* Aha, i realized, i have tons of rocks in my yard.

The person who both helped and taught me during this project, is a very intelligent man. One day in the beginning, he showed me drawings of bricks and how they had to be cut to fit in certain ways. i didn't understand a word that he said so i raised my hand and kept it there until he noticed. He asked, "What?" i replied, "i don't have a clue about what you are talking about. Show me so i can understand." He looked at me a little strangely from that point on, however, he was very patient with me throughout the two year project.

When we were ready for the fieldstones to be cemented on the outside of the brick furnace, that large, round, flat rock told me that it had to be placed in a very specific spot. i informed my mentor and, of course, he thought i was off my rocker, but he went with it. A few days later i heard some mumbling from the opposite side of the stove. i snuck around to see what was going on and there he was, talking to a rock, saying, "Ok, you can go there." i chuckled to myself. By the way, that flat rock is the first one people notice when they walk in the front door.

Once we were three quarters done, i felt confident enough to finish by myself. i was guided into some special effects at the top of the fireplace to allow the twelve inch floor joists to set right into the stove.

i was so proud of myself when my sister came to visit. It was her first time viewing my new fireplace. She walked over and stood in the front of the stove. She began crying. i asked what was going on. She pointed to the front of the fireplace where there were two pink stones.

When things happen, like trees or rocks talking, i have listened and followed their clues. Things may have turned out very differently had i not paid attention to their wisdom. Once these experiences happen with regularity, it is difficult to deny their validity. After a while events like this become common-place. New doorways seem to open up for us which actually play a part in directing our futures. Are you listening?

CHAPTER 8

Bring it
to the Table

i practiced Occupational Therapy for over thirty-five years. Besides this i hold a Masters in Rehabilitation Counseling. Both the fields of Rehabilitation Counseling and Occupational Therapy require and encourage addressing the whole being. Subsequently it was easy to slide into alternative types of therapies which support dialoguing as well as placing my hands on the bodies of my clients. Early on i realized, if i put my hands on someone and listened intently, that person would show, or tell me, what i was supposed to do.

Throughout my career i attended numerous workshops and trainings from Neuromuscular Techniques to Cranial Sacral Therapy to Zero Balance, Lymphatic Drainage, Visceral Manipulation and many more. i wanted a large bag of tools to be of service to a wide range of clientele. Instead of becoming certified in a specific modality, i opted for the eclectic approach.

My work has taken place in acute and general hospitals, rehabilitation facilities, psychiatric hospitals, skilled nursing facilities, home health agencies, privately owned programs, schools and my own private practice. i've created and implemented new programs across the country in many facilities and schools.

In this chapter I'd like to share a few of the cases i have witnessed and experienced. During my career as a therapist—some wild, unexpected and amazing things have presented themselves. All the names contained here are, of course, fictitious.

Man in a Coma

My first job as an Occupational Therapist took place at a community hospital in Southern California. During the first two months on the scene, i received a treatment order to perform 'range of motion' on Mr. Johnson, an older man in a coma. i went to his room and began moving his limbs around. It felt odd to work on someone who couldn't respond, so i started talking to him during the session. Every day for two or three weeks i performed the treatment and carried on a conversation with him as though he was present and aware.

One Friday afternoon, i saw an orderly wheeling Mr. Johnson out the door of the hospital on a gurney. i went over to find out what was going on. The orderly told me that the patient was being transferred to the nursing home down the street. i went to head of the gurney, put my hand gently on the man's shoulder and said, "Goodbye, Mr. Johnson." To our surprise, Mr. Johnson sat right up, said, "Thank you for talking with me." Then he lied down again as though nothing had happened; a man in a coma on a gurney. i almost fell over. How do you explain something like that?

The Girl in the Cage

i also worked with a group of teens locked up in an acute psychiatric hospital in Southern California. The schools, law enforcement agencies and parents didn't know what

87

to do with them, so they locked them away until the kids could act in an "appropriate manner." One of the activities i set up was a garden project where kids could earn 'privilege points' by working with me by pulling weeds and other various chores. They could then cash in earned points for special events or trips into the community with me. That way the kids could practice some of the skills they learned in my 'social skills' class.

One day while in the garden, a young girl confided in me. She told me that she was placed there because she 'dreamt things into reality.' She dreamt of someone being in an automobile accident, then that person was in an accident. She dreamed that her horse died, and, sure enough, a couple days later, the horse died. She truly believed that she caused these things to happen.

She also shared with me that a 'spirit man' visited her during many nights. He would stand by her bed and stare at her. She was afraid. i asked her a few questions about how this nightly visitor made her feel. i left her with some specific suggestions of things to try for the next time he came to visit her.

A few days later, the girl confided to me that her visitor had showed up again. He let her know that he was there to help. He said that her premonition dreams were actually a gift for her to help others in times of need. The girl's appearance changed so drastically from the frightened, self-tormented child that she didn't look anything like the same person anymore.

It never ceases to amaze me how 'understanding' can change and empower us. It is profound how one experience can alter our lives forever. Anyone who has had an 'out of the normal' event will certainly attest to this fact.

Oregon Hospice

The referral from the hospice unit read "Activities of Daily Living." The order for therapy was for Mrs. Carson, a patient diagnosed with cancer and not expected to live for more than a week. i visited Mrs. C each day for an hour or more. We practiced a number of daily living skills, but mostly we talked about her life. Quickly i grew more and more moved by this woman. She seemed to accept her dying with such grace and dignity.

One day i brought my flute into her room and played for about 5-7 minutes. Mrs. C sat quietly through my mini-concert of sad songs. After i finished she said, "That was lovely but, you know, I'm dying here. Do you think you could play something a little more lively?" We laughed. Before i left, she took my hand and thanked me for spending so much time with her. She appreciated our time together.

The following day on my way to her room, the charge nurse intercepted me. She told me that Mrs. Carson passed away early that morning. i walked into the conference room at the end of the hall, sat down and started to cry.

i felt as though i had just lost someone special. Across the parking lot i noticed a girl's elementary school. Some of the students were playing soccer in the field. As i watched them play, i thought about the woman who had just died.

Just then i heard a voice next to me saying, "i used to play like that when i was a young girl." i felt Mrs. C's presence as strongly as she were sitting right beside me. Then she said, "Come with me." Before i could think anything, we were flying up through the clouds and into the sunlight. i felt her convey her thanks to me at a very personal level. She told me that she 'had to go now.' Then she was gone.

Bang! i was right back in my body on a chair in the conference room looking out the window at the young girls on the soccer field. Tears streamed down my face, not from pain, but from the joy of the experience with this dying woman as she left the world for *who-knows-where.*

Three Little Shockers

One of my private clients, Linda, was diagnosed with cancer. Following surgery, she was left badly disfigured with some really nasty scars across her chest. During one of our therapy sessions she was lying on my treatment table when her face grew distorted. Within a few minutes her face grew ghostly pale and still. Even her chest stopped rising and falling. *"Holy shit,"* i thought,

"*She's dying right here on the table.*" Just as i was about to totally panic, i heard a little voice say, *Stay still. Hold this space.*

About ninety long seconds passed. Just then a glow surrounded her head; her face grew serene and peaceful as the color returned to her cheeks. She looked beautiful and radiant as she opened her eyes. She looked directly into my eyes and said, "i died. i was cut across my chest and i bled to death as if in another lifetime. i knew everything was going to be alright. Then i came back to life. i know that I'm going to live. i don't ever remember feeling this peaceful before."

Another client was on the table with his eyes closed. Everything was going along smoothly, then *Wham!* He started writhing in pain on the table. It looked and felt like he was being run over by a horse. Then he went dead still. This time i didn't panic – i simply watched and waited.

A few moments later his face began to radiate with a warm glow and a sense of peacefulness. His eyes bolted open and he blurted out, "No wonder why I'm so afraid of horses. i was stomped to death by one. i was actually dead then someone told me i had to go back and finish what i came here for, whatever that is."

A third person, a female, was on the table when she went into a flailing motion that looked like drowning.

Grasping for something above her and gasping for air, she went totally limp and gray.

Again, there was no respiration and/or movement on her part.

By now i was getting used to these intense situations, so i just held the space. After a moment or two, she grew all glowy and peaceful. She opened her eyes and stated, "i drowned. That's why i have been so afraid of the water all my life. i must learn how to swim."

Mongolian Murder

Mic lied down on the table. Within five minutes she and i went into the following experience. We were in a truly darkened landscape – the words *Outer Mongolia* kept fluttering through my mind.

Bound and lying on the ground, she was surrounded by a number of hooded monks. They were disemboweling her, nailing her entrails to the ground all around her. They were chanting something and filling her whole being with fear. i was an old man nearby who was forced to watch this event. They warned her never to speak of the knowledge of God or there would be dire consequences. Then she died.

Mic came out of the treatment immediately. She wanted to know if i was there with her – yes, i nodded. She said she finally knew why she felt that something really bad

would happen to her if she ever told anyone anything about God. For the longest time she has never said anything to anyone about her religion and/or God because of this powerful fear that she may be killed. Now she knew why.

The Reiki Master

On a late Sunday afternoon i received a phone call from a friend asking if i would please do a treatment with her Reiki Master. The last thing i wanted was to work that late on a Sunday. However, she pleaded and i relented.

When they came to the house i was shocked how weak this elderly woman looked. She appeared completely depleted of energy and ready for the grave at any moment. This was no problem though, as i was getting accustomed to people dying on the table – *what the heck!* Before getting on the table, she showed me a picture of an older man. She said, "This is the doctor i used to work with. He's dead. He is going to help you work with me. "*Okay,* i thought; *this is going to be interesting.*

During the next two and a half hours, i sensed the presence of a man in the room hovering over the woman. i heard little nudges telling me to' put my hands here' or 'this place is important, keep your hands here while i do something'. A number of times i noticed an increase in the flow of heat and energy stream through my hands. When the session was over, the woman

literally jumped off the table and gave me a nice, warm hug. Full of life, she radiated a palpable aura that filled the room, looking nothing like the woman who walked into my house a few hours earlier.

That was my first conscious co-treatment session with someone not in a physical body. Amazing!

My Friend

i have a friend whom i treated whenever he felt the need for a session. At this particular time he was losing weight drastically and seriously worried about his health. Once on the table we started the session.

Within moments i was transported to the steps of a Buddhist temple during the 13th century (Persia, i think). We were child students together. We had been up and down those hundreds of steps a thousand times if once. He was the more serious one when it came to studies while i was the imp.

Then the scene changed to years later. We were men. We had spent our lives together at the temple, the closest of friends. He was sick. In fact, i was holding him in my arms as he was dying. Just then i popped back into my body in my treatment room. Again, i was holding my friend as he seemed to be dying. Waves of love mixed with grief washed through me. i didn't want to tell him what i had just experienced for fear that it may influence his future.

After the treatment he told me that he was leaving the state soon. i was concerned that i would never see him again.

About six months later, i saw him at a seminar. He looked to be the picture of health. He told me that a few months after our last meeting he found himself in a nursing home. Wasted away to less than 90 pounds, and in diapers, he had been given up for dead by the medical staff. He then spoke of an inner experience where he was given the opportunity to avert his impending death. Sure enough, there he was, 125 pounds of living flesh, smiling from ear to ear and beaming from within – my friend from the past.

i bow to the power and resilience of the human spirit.

The Kid

i answered the door to meet my new client, a young man in his twenties. i invited him to sit on the table and asked how he found me and what was he doing here. He said that someone, he couldn't remember who, gave him my number and urged him to call. He wasn't sure why he was there but he knew that 'he had to come.' He explained that, at 26 years old, he was being groomed to become a leader of his religion.

He laid down on the table. As soon as i put my hands on him a number of beings in hazy forms appeared in the room.

They looked a little like Crosby, Stills & Nash, with long hair and beards. They instructed me what to do and where to put my hands.

A few moments into the treatment they informed me that they were members of the "White Brotherhood." They were going to take over this young man's spiritual training. i was to tell the kid to stop studying his religious works because he was to learn a different way. i promptly informed them that i would do no such thing. The lad would think me nuts. How would that go over if people found out i was telling individuals to give up their methods of religious training? It wouldn't be long before i'd end up a clientless therapist.

They persisted for an hour as i worked on the boy. Finally i assented and let the kid know. He was stunned by this information. He wanted me to tell him what to do, so, i gave him my five minute dissertation on living a spiritually oriented lifestyle. It went something like this. *Should you choose this path, you will experience both great joys and possibly times of utter despair to the point where you wonder why you ever chose this way. i have known both and yet, i would again and again choose the way of spirit.*

We finished the session. He told me that he could only pay half of my fee, promising to bring me the rest. *Oh well, it's not really about just the money now, is it?*

Two days later, he arrived at my door to pay the remainder and thanked me for the talk on the 'spiritual life.' He stated that his aunts and uncles have always told him that he was going grow up to make changes in the world. Now he knew a new direction for himself.

i am quite certain that the boys 'in the hood' (White Brotherhood that is) were snickering at this whole event. Either way i looked at it, it was amazing being a channel for something so special.

The Priestess and the Way Station

Sitting on the edge of a canyon located deep in the southwestern U.S., i met a woman named Char. We struck up a conversation centered round our 'out of the ordinary' experiences. Both of us worked on people, so we agreed to meet for a treatment swap.

A week or so later, we met. She hopped up on the table first. Within one minute of putting my hands on her i was transported to a room with a marble floor (the pattern was so striking that i drew it on paper following the session). The woman in the room was a high priestess. She was surrounded by a number of male priests who were in the process of killing her. Before clubbing her to death, they told her that she 'knew too much' for a woman and a priestess. She could not be allowed to live.

Once they started beating her, Char's eyes popped open.

She stated more than asked, "You were there and saw the whole thing." We chatted a bit about the significance of the experience and how it tied into her present day life. We set a date for the next meeting.

During the second session, she was sitting on a marble bench on a stair landing between floors. Conversing with a wise man, her master, she was pleading with him not to leave her. The master tried to tell her that it was time for him to go; she really didn't need him anymore. There would be another master coming along that would take her to the next phase in her training.

While observing this scene i felt a pull to go up the stairs. Following the urge, i walked up and entered some kind of station. Surrounded by a glass-like enclosed gigantic room, i observed beings floating above the floor while moving in certain directions. i watched them entering and leaving through the glass doorways, much like a bus or train station. i knew, that this was a 'way station' for souls going to different worlds or parts of this world.

i returned to physical consciousness at the exact same time that Char did. She validated the meeting between her and the inner master. She told me that deep inside she knew that it was time to move on, however, she loved him so much that she just didn't want it to come to an end. i told her of my visiting the way station. She knew of its existence.

It was my turn. During my session i found myself in an unfamiliar building which i knew to be a church or temple. i entered. On each side of the main aisle pews faced the central corridor. A number of 'non-humans' in dark brown, hooded robes occupied the seats. They appeared to be some type of reptilian creatures. i immediately thought of the word *Lizzies*. They stared at me as i walked down the aisle.

i entered a special room off to the side of the main hall. Inside i spotted a contraption in the middle of the room. It looked like a 'stubbie' lazer set upon a post. A ball of light appeared in the top of the thing then shot through a portal in one of the walls. Then, it adjusted itself and shot another ball of light through a different hole in the wall. i had the sense that the balls of light were souls being sent to pre-determined places. Once i realized this i returned to my body lying on the table. i was left with the feeling that the *Lizzies* were not very loving beings.

Slaves

i met a woman at a seminar named J. After chatting for a few minutes, i felt an inner nudge to perform a certain kind of treatment with her. However, before i had dared bring it up, she left. She returned a short time later to ask me about a particular performance being held in the program. Unexpectedly, i began firing some heavy questions at her and she answered each one of them without missing a beat. All of a sudden she squared off in front of me with hands on her hips as if to demand,

"What are you going to do?" i said, "My intuition is guiding me to provide you with a certain kind of treatment. She replied, "Fine. When?"

We met later that day for the session. Within five minutes of my touching her, we found ourselves transported to a shack on a southern plantation. J., a slave lying on a bed delivering a child, was in agony. Also a slave, i was aware that i was her husband. The infant was white. Once the birthing process was over, the owner of the plantation (a white man with blond hair) whisked the newborn baby away. The mother and i were unable to do anything but to watch this man, our master, take the child.

That ended the treatment session. Once fully returned to the room, J. confirmed that we had both experienced the same scenario.

Liz on the Table

While giving a treatment to my sister Liz, her eyes suddenly began to flicker beneath closed lids. After a few moments her body went icy cold. While in the experience she started talking about being under the surface and watching her dogs go down into the depths of the frigid water as they drowned. She tried her best yet couldn't save them even though she attempted to follow after them in her heavy winter coat. She opened her eyes and stated, "that's why i have the sled."

On her garage wall is a full-sized dog sled that she 'had to have' but has never used. For a period of time Liz has been the owner of a number of Malamute dogs.

During another session, Liz experienced fighting in a war. She was a captain in an army; our other sister, Laura, was a sergeant who had served with her in many battles. Liz remarked about how she trusted Laura with her life. On numerous occasions, Laura had saved her life and/or protected her from harm.

After the session, Liz stated that she now understood the nature of her relationship with her older sister. She also remarked how Laura could always be counted on no matter what the circumstances.

Is it a fact that we have been with our family members before? Do we agree to be together again and again out of love or to complete some past issues or karmic situations that need working out? When events like the preceding experiences occur again and again, it becomes difficult to deny their reality. Once open to them, possibilities can, and do, exist never before present in our fields of vision.

CHAPTER 9

My Time on the Table

Throughout the years, i've had many treatment sessions from a number of different people from all walks of life. i cannot possibly remember even half of them so i have selected a few that jump out at me. i am choosing hands-on events from licensed therapists as opposed to astrologers, psychic readers and those who channel. However, these latter elements seep into some of the sessions; that is the nature of working 'on the fringe'. The most important thing to remember, i think, is how the information during each session ties into the reality of everyday living. Again, the names of those involved have been altered.

An Earthquake in Oregon

Sometime in the late 70s or early 80s a good friend of mine was living in Oregon. i drove up from California for a visit. She suggested to me that while in the area, i should see this woman who does massage and other 'interesting stuff.' As my friend was a well-known astrologer, i trusted her judgment when it came to areas that i didn't know.

Once the time was set, my friend gave me directions and i arrived for my appointment. The woman appeared normal; maybe a little hippie-ish. Many of us looked that way. Her massage room was in the back yard in an out-building. The season was in between the time of year the temperature could be either comfortably warm, or uncomfortably cold and damp. That day the temperature was about 45 degrees F, cold and damp.

As soon as she began the massage my body began to emit unbelievable amounts of heat. After fifteen minutes the room was nice and toasty. She began telling me that i had been selected to carry some kind of information into the world. When the time was right, it would simply happen – i didn't have to do anything at all. Now we were getting a little strange but not way out there.

The room grew hotter and hotter. She said that a strong and powerful force ran through me. At that very instant the ground began to rumble, shaking the little out-building. It felt like the seismic event punctuated her statement. When all grew still she remarked that i should be very careful about using this kind of power. OK, i was a tad disturbed by all this.

i didn't understand what the whole experience meant, yet i knew it wasn't necessary to know. That happened eons ago. Today i know more about myself, however, numerous experiences continue to be completely beyond my understanding. And that is OK.

On the Rack

My friend, Kate, was a physical therapist. We attended a few therapy workshops together to learn different ways to treat tissues. We had become good friends and would work on each other on occasion.

One day she was working on my chest when i dropped into an experience where i was being held down on some kind of wooden platform. People in brown robes were torturing me. i saw medieval looking gadgets and ropes tied to my wrists and ankles. A big wheel turned, stretching my limbs apart. i knew i was in great pain but couldn't feel a thing. The robed characters were saying, or chanting, something designed to raise the level of fear into different parts of my being.

Of course, i verbalized this entire event as it happened. When i slid back into my body and opened my eyes, i could tell that my friend was quite shocked by the experience. Her eyes were the size of golf balls. She had never taken part in a treatment quite like this one.

East Meets West

Following a recommendation from a good friend, i scheduled an appointment with a Chinese Medicine practitioner who had been cross-trained with a group of southwestern Native Shaman. When we introduced ourselves, i saw a jungle-green pyramid directly over his shoulder. *Whoa, this is gonna be interesting*, i thought.

During the first few moments of the treatment i inwardly saw a few brown robed individuals. *Red Flag! Brown Robes, more torture!* Immediately i recognized one of them; a spiritual traveler i knew. i greeted him warmly, knowing that his presence there was solely for my benefit. i relaxed instantly.

A few minutes later, i saw the doc's entire chakra system light up in brilliant magenta as it aligned with my system of beautiful, sky blue. When they overlapped, the color changed to a cobalt bluish purple – the blend i knew to be my own color ray. i was enraptured by the aliveness of the colors and the high vibratory rate. The sight was magnificent.

Our chakra systems separated leaving me in a very elevated state. A few short moments passed. Then a glowing, golden statue of Buddha moved into and settled into my inner space. My eyes filled with tears of joy as i felt completely whole and fulfilled.

Following the session, the doc told me some profound statements referring to what he thought about my life path. Needless to say, my drive home was in an altered state. All the while i kept wondering, *what is really possible? Who are we, really?*

The Blue Angel

About ten years ago i attended an advanced therapy workshop on the coast of California. We were grouped together for multi-hand intensive sessions. Some of the treatments focused on our own birthing processes and other life experiences that had been locked away somewhere in our bodies.

i arrived at the site bringing with me space a kidney infection and prescription medication.

A low grade temperature, plus aches and pains, were symptoms of the infection. At my turn on the table, five therapists worked on me for two hours or more. At some point i began screaming, "i hate this body. i hate being human and having to deal with this shit." My temperature rose sharply, my kidney burned with pain and i was writhing wildly on the table dragging all five therapists along with me.

In the middle of the mayhem, i heard one of the therapists say, "There is a blue angel here. i haven't seen him since i was a little boy. He's beautiful." At that very moment i surrendered. Somehow i knew that the kidney infection was symptomatic of the anger i held inside of me. Just then, the burning pain and temperature went away. i felt a sense of peace wash through me calming my entire body.

Convinced that my kidney infection was gone, i recall lying on the table thinking, *how could this be*? *This is a medical anomaly. How do the emotions create such imbalance and sickness within our bodies*? Sure enough, the kidney infection had cleared up right there on the table. Later on, i threw the meds away.

White Horse

i attended another therapeutic program, one in which horses were an integral part of the therapy process. We placed a treatment table in the paddock and carried on sessions with two horses which were free to come and

go as they pleased. Sometimes one of them would get involved in the session; other times they stayed at a distance. Most of the time, however, both horses paid attention to what was happening on the table.

My time came to 'be the client.' Before i reached within 100 yards from the paddock, i began crying profusely. i experienced an overwhelming sense of gratitude. By the time i was led into the paddock, my face and the front of my shirt were soaked. The therapist facilitating the session asked me what was wrong. i said, "Absolutely nothing – just gratitude."

He asked me to close my eyes while he placed his hand on my thorax (chest) above my heart. He was talking but i couldn't hear a word. i felt one of the horses touch my heart then slobbered my entire face. Before i had time enough to think, *Great*, i started inwardly seeing bears and hundreds of horses running side by side on an open plane right there in the paddock. i began to verbalize what i was witnessing. i felt the guy's hand tremble on my chest.

After a few moments, everything went dead quiet. In my inner vision, i saw the most magnificent white stallion i have ever seen coming out of the clouds, heading directly towards me. The tears rolled down my face again. The horse told me that, *It was OK to use my natural power now. He and the power would always be there for me to draw upon.*

Through my tears, i felt a sense of honor blended with gratitude and pure, clean love. This touched the very core of my being.

i opened my eyes. The guy holding me was also crying, as was the other therapist with us in the paddock. i felt so moved and high that i couldn't talk to or be around anyone for over an hour. i found a small garden area to sit quietly amongst the flowers and contemplate what had just happened .

Considerations

Whether or not we are aware of the significance of these "unexplainable" events that happen to us, the fact is: they happen. The mere existence of such happenings changes our beliefs of who, or what, we think we are. To me, they are adventures. The more i accept them, the more real and exciting my life becomes. Why try to stop, or explain away, the show we're in when we are paying the admission fees anyway?

CHAPTER 10

Native Americans

For the major part of my life, feeling safe in the woods whether alone or with a number of people is natural for me. The same holds true with canoes. When traveling rivers or lakes by canoe or kayak, i am comfortable sitting in the rear of the craft with an oar or paddle in my hands. As i scan the water ahead i sense a knowledge and awareness that i assume come from a past life. My life is so rich with many such experiences, that i'm not exactly sure where to start.

My First Kiva

During my first journey into the American Southwest, i was determined to see all the big sights like the Grand Canyon, Carlsbad Caverns, Yellowstone, etc. When i visited Mesa Verde, i was fascinated with the cliff dwellings – something awakened in me. Excited i climbed down the ladder into the kiva. i seemed to know what the ranger was going to talk about before he opened his mouth. i also knew that most of the 'life energy' had been sucked out of the kiva by thousands of tourists' visits. i was a bit disappointed. *There must be something more*, i thought.

In a different area (still in the park, i think), i found another kiva. With no one else around and, a ladder inviting me to explore, i could not resist climbing down into this one. This kiva was alive, humming with energy. i noticed a hole in one of the walls where the shaman must have experienced their visions. Of course, i crawled into the hole and closed my eyes. *Holy shit!*

Images flew to me at an incredible speed–some of them psychically intense and much more than i could handle.

i had tapped into something for which i definitely was not prepared. It shook me so much that i flew up that ladder, jumped in the car and drove away as fast as i could. Too scared, i did not approach another kiva for another twelve years.

Chief Joseph and the Nez Perce

i found myself in an LA office waiting with my wife for an appointment she made with a psychic reader. A man walked in, looked straight at me and said, "Where have you been? Come into my office." i followed, wondering what was going on, because my wife had made an appointment for "us" to see him, not just me.

As soon as i sat down, he began rattling off details about past lives and my being taught by inner masters. He said that he didn't care if i were run over by a Mack truck; i would live for a long time because a great Native American chief is protecting me. "What?" i asked. "Who is it?" He replied, "You'll find out soon."*Great,* i thought. *Now what?*

Six months later i was planning to move north to Oregon, alone. My plan was to settle in and prepare for my kids to spend the summer with me. Before i left the LA area, i received an invitation to a customer's home. On one of her walls, i saw a picture of a Native American chief

painted on a wooden serving tray. i couldn't move; my feet froze to the floor, my skin goose-bumped and tears filled my eyes. i opened my mouth – out popped the words, "That's him, who is he?" "Why, that's Chief Joseph," she told me. "He was the leader of the Nez Perce tribe in Oregon." i was beside myself; i left and went straight to the library.

i discovered that Chief Joseph Senior and Junior were prominent figures of the Nez Perce Indians who lived in southwestern Oregon among the Wallowa Mountains. i knew immediately that i needed to visit that area before starting a new life as a single parent. My whole life had changed; and i was primed for a new adventure.

Driving an old beat up 1966 Plymouth Valiant (one of the few remnants from my marriage) i headed north. Outside of Boise, Idaho the car overheated, so i pulled into a local park for a nap and a chance to let the vehicle cool down.

As soon as my eyes closed, i entered a Technicolor-like dream. As a young native warrior, i was lifting my woman onto a horse, sending her away from trouble in the camp. Sometime in the recent past, we had taken part in some kind of 'joining ceremony'. The dream was so clear and real, her face so familiar, that it spooked me a bit. i hopped back in the Valiant and continued driving north.

That night i pulled off the interstate and onto a winding road heading north for the town of Joseph, Oregon. For the next fifty or so miles, an old Native man kept appearing in the back seat of the car; his presence was strong. At one point he said, "Welcome home, my son." My whole body chilled and tears started pouring down my face. After nearly an hour of this, i could not take it anymore. i pulled off to the side of the road and climbed a small hill with my dog, Angel.

Once on top i saw the surrounding mountains lit by the stars of the Milky Way. i was definitely shaken by these events. Wondering if i was nuts, i stood there staring at the mountains and the sky. As i turned towards the car, two meteorites blazed across the sky. *Ok, that's enough. i'm going to sleep now.* i went back to the car to spend the night sleeping right there in the front seat.

Upon waking, i drove to the small town of Joseph. i found a breakfast place and heard about the local museum of the Nez Perce. That sounded like a good place to start. Just inside the door of the museum was a real tepee and a number of artifacts, but what caught my attention was a series of pictures on the wall. i stood in front of one and, *Wham!* My feet were frozen to the floor, goose-bumps erupted all over me, and a flood of tears streamed down my face. A painting displayed a young brave lifting a woman onto a horse: exactly as i had seen the day before in my dream. The next few pictures told the story of the trouble in the camp. *OK, something is happening – i need to go outside.*

An hour or so later, i found a campground by Wallowa Lake. i parked the car and took a badly needed walk into the woods. i kept feeling a strong presence as though someone was walking right next to me. i hoped that this 'whomever' would appear and state their business. Finally, at the end of my waning patience, i blurted out, "Ok, i've had it. Look, i know you're here. Just show yourself – a deer, a squirrel – i don't give a damn. Tell me what you want; tell me anything." Nothing.

More than a little disheveled, i drove back to town and strode into the town saloon for a beer or two. As i sat on a bar stool wondering, *what the hell is going on,* i looked up from the bar noticing a calendar from 1978. i realized that whatever happened here that was connected to me, did so about a century ago. Everywhere i went in this little town, i expected to see that woman in the vision and the painting to appear right before me at any moment.

Ok, i thought, all this happened about 100 years ago. *Why i needed to come here, i had no idea.* My marriage and family life were over; i must be in shock and psychologically unstable. i'll go to Portland, start a new life and get myself back together again. Within hours i left Joseph.

On the major highway west, the old Valiant started overheating again. i exited the main road, figuring that i would get something to eat while the car cooled down. i found a diner, went in, sat down at the counter and

ordered a burger and fries to ground me. Feeling better, i paid the bill and headed for the door. On the wall beside the door was a painting of the woman i had placed on the horse in my dream. i jumped in the car and drove to Portland, believing that i had indeed, lost my mind.

Almost ten years later, i made the trip north to Portland in order to visit a friend. On the return trip we stopped at a restaurant off Highway 5. The host led us to a table. On the wall above our table was the same painting of the woman i put on the horse in my vision. This restaurant was at least 100 miles from the diner i stopped in ten years prior. i purchased the piece and to this day it hangs on my living room wall.

Over the years i have returned to a number of spots where the Nez Perce have camped, including their last stand in the Bear Paws Mountains in eastern Montana. At each and every spot i have experienced something extraordinary. Each event started with my feet being frozen in place, goose bumps invading my entire body and tears flooding down my face. Every experience has been just as real to me as everyday life. Who is to say that i wasn't glimpsing one of my own past life times? Who can judge such occurrences?

Flute at the Cliff Dwelling

i hiked into the desert canyon to an Anasazi cliff dwelling well off the beaten path. Right around dusk i entered one of the dwellings with my silver, metal flute. i sat

down in a room that felt like a special gathering place resplendent with marks and symbols painted on the wall.

As i warmed up, the birds outside started actively chatting and chirping up a storm in a rhythm that rang throughout the small canyon, as if responding to the notes of the flute. A few moments later, i felt a strong presence in the room. i closed my eyes and continued to play. Immediately i began envisioning a number of old native men sitting in a circle around me. Some of them had head dresses and others were plainly clad in deerskin-looking outfits. All of them appeared to be ancient. Mentally i said to them, *Excuse me for my terrible playing; if you want me to play something, please show me or play through me.*

i began fingering a tune i had never played before – a song foreign to my limited repertoire. By the time i finished i *knew* (not just thought) that i had been altered by the song and presence of these beings. i crawled out of the room with a new sense of respect and wonder for the tribal ways of the southwestern natives. Sleeping was difficult for the rest of the night.

About two to three months later a friend gave me a cassette tape of Native American Flute music entitled, "Gathering of the Shamans." She informed me that i needed the tape; for whatever reason, she knew not. One of the songs was the same tune i had played in the cliff dwelling. What a shock!

Native Patient

While working as a therapist in a Montana hospital, i received a referral to evaluate a patient who recently suffered from a stroke. i entered the room and located my client who was an eighty-something-year-old Native American woman. Her long white hair and weathered dark skin gave her a look of ancient wisdom.

After a short moment i detected that she couldn't talk or sit or stand without help. While i gestured her through a brief evaluation, i couldn't help but notice that she consistently stared at an area just above my head.

Over the next week, she gradually regained sensation and movement in her body and began speaking a few words in her native tongue. It certainly wasn't English. During each and every visit she kept looking at something above my head. i thought the cerebral event (stroke) must have affected her eye sight or mentation. She appeared to enjoy our meetings – she kept smiling at me and doing everything i asked of her.

A few days later she was due to be discharged to her daughter's home. i scheduled a meeting with her daughter in order to go over her mom's care and home exercise program. They patiently waited while i went through my routine. The daughter asked some very relevant and intelligent questions about her mom's status and prognosis.

When i finished, the older woman made some kind of demand of her daughter. They had a little 'discussion' for a moment or two. The younger of the two faced me saying that her mother wanted to tell me something. She translated, "Ever since i appeared at her bedside, she has been seeing a great Native American chief above my head. The spirit chief told her to do everything i told her to do." She also instructed her daughter to give me an item. The woman gave her mother a bag, out of which, the old woman retrieved a hand-braided strand of sweet grass. The daughter explained to me that, in her culture, when someone gives a white person 'sacred sage', it is a very important gesture of thanks.

The old woman presented me with the sage and hugged me warmly. Tears filled my eyes as i accepted both gifts. It is beyond me how or why this happened. i was left with a deep sense of gratitude for the experience.

Vortex and Ancient Tools

My woman and i camped at one of my favorite spots deep in a canyon overlooking a river in south central Utah. That night we had a discussion about why she was unable to feel energy in her hands. She was aware of the energy all around her but she just couldn't feel it.

The next day we were to drive to Lake Powell. i didn't want to drive back to the freeway, so i checked my trusty gazette for a back road to a different place on the highway.

Finding a passable route (during storms, they are not), we headed out.

About thirty minutes into the drive, we came upon a small mesa. A strong energy emitted from this hill top, and when we drove around its base, the force grew in power. i tried to ignore it because i wanted to get to Powell. As i drove away, a booming voice inside of me screamed, *Stop now, you must go to the top of the mesa. OK*, i turned around and parked the truck.

i climbed out of the vehicle and prepared to ascend the hill. i gazed to the top and instantly knew that something profound was awaiting us. You know what i mean - that sense of anticipation that doesn't go away. It felt like a big, powerful vortex was drawing us to the top of the mesa.

Once on the rim, we discovered an odd-shaped hole surrounded by rocks both rounded and flat. My woman felt something tingling in her hands for the first time in her life. She wanted to stay right there. i needed to walk around, and left her at the hole for about thirty minutes. The wind increased and swirled around the top of the mesa, actually forming a vortex. Swept up by its energy, i found myself in a heightened state of awareness.

i heard the 'Ancient Ones' all around me. They were speaking in a tongue unknown to me, however, it translated in my head to something like, *We are giving you these ancient tools. You have earned them. You will*

know each one when it is time for you to use them. i envisioned oddly shaped items hung in the sky, taken down and placed into my auric space. By the time i finished the circuit, i felt elated, honored and grateful for this development. Who am i to be part of this amazing event? Were they the same ancient beings from the cliff dwelling?

i found my woman at the same spot i left her. Sitting on a rock and white as a ghost, she described the tingling in her hands; how it grew until an intense energy spread through her entire body making her tremble and shake. She was crying tears of gratefulness and awe.

Whatever it was, the experience on the mesa changed us both in our own separate ways. i believe that event was a turning point in her life. A few years later, she returned to school to become a massage therapist.

The Only Apache Around

i wanted to investigate this particular kind of house construction (dome, or sand bag house) in a town near Tucson, Arizona. Easily enough i found the little town yet needed some help locating the buildings. My friend advised me to stop at the artist store for directions. When i asked the Native American man sitting behind the desk, he stood right up and said that he must take me there himself. He was looking at me a little strangely, but that happens frequently – no big deal.

On the way, the man stated, "i don't know why i am telling you this, but i am the only pure Apache who lives here. When you showed up, i knew i had to guide you to this special place." i expressed to him that i understand such things and that i, too, recognized something about him also. We chatted a bit about the possibility of knowing each other during some other time.

Once there, we both knew that his task was over. We shook hands and parted. The dome houses were very cool and creative. The owner informed me that ten acres on this spot were for sale. Right in the middle of the property was a natural medicine wheel. i had absolutely no idea how i knew that, but i did. i sat on a large rock and started chanting, slipping into a state of contemplation.

A few moments later, i was smack in the middle of a massacre. There was blood everywhere – on the ground, on the rocks – everywhere ran blood. i couldn't tell whether it was white men or red killed, but it felt like the land still held the memory and energy of that terrible event.

Why did i experience this? Why did the Apache 'need' to take me there? These questions may never provide the answers i want. Needless to say, i didn't buy the ten acres. To this day, every time i drive through that area, i shed a few tears. Had i lived through this massacre like i had with the Nez Perce or simply heard the voices of those gone by, or the cry of the land?

A Few Thoughts

From my experiences and readings, i find that some of my own natural behaviors are much like those typically found in the Native American culture. Greeting my ancestors and the directions of the earth each day, thanking the life forms that die for my nourishment or feeling 'in tune' with natural environs are quite similar to their ways. After catching me doing my morning greetings one day, my father commented to me that, of all the kids, cousins and grandchildren, i was the one who seemed most like his native grandmother.

CHAPTER 11

Deaths and Funerals

Since my grandfather's death when i was twelve, deaths and funerals have taken on a particular kind of significance. One never knows what is going to take place when a family member dies. People may say or do things that are out of character for them.

Following a close one's passing, or translation, means that we are left with the task of re-defining who and what we are without that person in our lives. We are no longer a son or a daughter simply because that role is gone, never to return. That, however, is after the funeral ritual is over. This chapter is mostly concerned with the actual death and the funerals of some of my family members.

Grammy's Final Goodbye

At Grammy's church service i told a story about my dad's mother. i remembered as a young boy feeding her dog, Gypsy, dog bones and dried apricots in her doghouse – one for her and one for me. i actually liked both; and so did she. When we ran out, i would sneak into the house and take some more. Every time the box of apricots or bones grew empty, a new box magically appeared with the top pried open so all i had to do was grab some and slink out the back door. It wasn't until years later that Grammy told me the truth.

My grandmother's funeral was held on a sunny, windless afternoon. Not a hint of breeze was in the air. i was standing next to my aunt when my attention was pulled

upwards to the tops of a few fir trees. A puff of wind bent the tops over. i knew, somehow, that it was her. Her spirit passed right through my aunt, then me, and finally took off into the sky and away.

My aunt looked as if she had just seen a ghost. With an astonished look upon her face, she said to me, "That was my mother, wasn't it?" i smiled and let it go. Later on at the family gathering she cornered me for a little 'discussion.' For the first time in her life, my aunt glimpsed something beyond her sense of reality; something that before this experience, was completely unbelievable to her.

My Mother

My mother and i were close. i wrote to her no matter where i was--Vietnam, California, everywhere. Besides keeping in contact, i visited whenever i could. When she developed arthritis, i arrived every June to turn over the ground for her summer gardens. Some of our best chats were at 5 a.m. over coffee before others were awake. Having delivered and raised six children, mornings were her rare and only quiet times of the day. i treasured those moments with her.

My older sister called from Miami. Our mother was in the hospital and not doing well. As a nurse well acquainted with sickness and trauma, my sister let us know this might be our last chance to see her and that we should travel to Miami right away. i contacted my

younger brother and sister and within hours we were in my truck leaving Maine on our way to Miami. We arrived a day later at the hospital.

The attending physician informed me of the seriousness of my mom's condition. He expected her to die within 24-48 hours and recommended that i gather the family members together to decide whether or not to let my mother die naturally or keep her technically alive with the aid of machines. With much discussion and emotion, we decided to let her go on her own.

i sat on the edge of her bed holding her hand and talking when she experienced a seizure-like event. When she came out of it, she looked deeply into my eyes and asked, "Bobby, am i going to die now?" i replied, "Yes, ma, i think so. The doctor says that you have a day or so." She went quiet for a moment or so then asked me to bring everyone into the room. She requested that we leave for the day because she wanted to be alone.

When we returned early the next morning, she was unconscious during her last moments. One final gasp of breath and she was gone. i took my dad by the arm and led him outside. Standing in the parking lot by a coconut palm, for some strange reason, i asked him to give me a boost so i could climb up into the tree. i picked two coconuts and dropped them down to him. He took the nuts to the car while i went to sit down by the water. Looking out over the bay, i realized that i was born less than a mile away.

Recalling my mother's last few days in the hospital, i suddenly felt her presence next to me, surrounding and filling me at the same time. i knew she was there to say goodbye. Instead of pain and grief all i could feel was love. A moment or two passed - i can never really tell during these experiences. i felt her leave me and sensed, more than saw her, fly out over the water and into the clouds. i wondered why most people don't experience this personal type of parting as her goodbye seemed normal and natural. i sat there for a while staring out over the bay.

My Father

My dad was a grand prankster and i was always trying to outdo him, but somehow fell short. Not many people understood the way we communicated with each other. We could stay up all night playing cards or backgammon for money, cursing at each other with ferocity and enjoying every minute of it.

i vividly remember his being hospitalized in Michigan for a surgical bypass. i drove straight through from Utah crying and hoping all the way that he wouldn't die before i got there. Looking like i had driven all night i walked into the hospital room. There he was, alive and grinning while lying in bed surrounded by a few sisters and a brother.

The first thing out of his mouth was, "What are you doing here?" i replied, "i was in the neighborhood and

heard you were in here, so i figured that i'd stop by and say hi." His immediate response was, "Cash or check?" i volleyed with, "You know me, i always like it green." My siblings were appalled by our banter, but that's the way we liked it. *Oh, well.*

When my mom died, my father came to live with me in many different places. We traveled extensively; he slept in the bed in the camper and i, the tent. In those instances when our talks would turn to his dying. i told him that i would try to help him 'cross over'. i let him know that i would do everything i could to be with him at that moment. i gave him a special word to chant when he left his body. He eyed me strangely but said he would give it a shot.

When my nephew called to say that my dad had passed away, i immediately sat down on the couch and began to chant. Within a moment or two i was traveling through a darkened sky. i saw my father in the distance standing with someone i knew. i felt myself wanting to go to him but a gentle voice beside me said, *Wait here.*

Out of the nothingness my mother appeared and approached the two figures. Inside i heard her ask the other figure if she could take my dad across the river of death – she had been waiting for him.

Before they disappeared, the three of them generated a powerful feeling of love that filled the entire area – a beautiful and uplifting sight!

Suddenly, back in my body sitting on the couch, a sense of joy and wonderment filled my being completely. How could i possibly feel sadness after such an event ?

My father translated from this life over fifteen years ago. To this day i have never felt the need to cry over my dad's passing. When tears do come, it's because i miss my old traveling buddy, my dad.

CHAPTER 12

Thoughts, Questions and Considerations

By now you can tell that quite a number of unusual, varied and surprising events make up a significant part of my life experience. Every one of these occurrences is a true story; they actually did happen. It would take a wild and out of control imagination to create stories like the ones i have told in this book. However, over the years, i made a habit of writing down many personal experiences simply because they were different from normal, everyday events. For example, how many times does one receive communiques from animals, plants, other mammals, minerals or people who no longer inhabit a physical body? i knew these experiences were unusual and my conclusion is that i led an interesting life filled with many wild and exciting events. For that, i am thankful.

These varied and odd happenings have caused my mind to wondering: who are we? What is our role on this planet as one of its species? Why and how can individuals who have died continue to speak with us? How could a dolphin possibly speak with me in English and direct me to enhance healing processes in other humans? How is it that we can communicate with our pets, plants or our loved ones after they have left this world? Do trees and rocks have consciousness capable of conveying thoughts and ideas to human beings and other species? Is all Life around us talking? You know, i believe that IT is!

Throughout my life i have thought of myself as a logical and reasoning person.

From kindergarten to completion of a Masters' program, i have learned to look at things objectively. Most of the teaching has served me well. However, i've struggled with the objective part from an early age. No one ever taught me that i could see or hear a dead person like my grandfather at his death. Family, friends and teachers consistently discouraged me from believing that animals could communicate with us. Yet i always knew what my dogs needed or wanted. How on earth did our dog, King, know to drag my four-year old sister out of the street when she was in danger?

During the therapy curriculum in college the concept of 'objectivity' was drilled into us. i remember one class when i challenged the professor on the topic. She stated that it was of the utmost importance for a clinician to remain objective and detached emotionally at all times when with a patient. i disagreed with her saying that unless clients actually 'feel' that we are with them, there will be no real therapeutic rapport. i understood the idea that, as a therapist, we would be more proficient if not emotionally overwhelmed or overly sympathetic with each client's process. However, i knew there needed to be balance; a space where i could stay present for the client and yet not thrown off kilter by their disease or trauma.

Applying that same balance to life around me in general has made for a certain quality of life. Intuition and insight, combined with reason, have earned their places as some of the most important instruments for my

professional and personal life. At times, however, intuition and insight rule out over reason, leading me to unexpected or unusual experiences. The more i attend to inner sight and hearing, the more worlds open to me. i am convinced that we possess capabilities for much more than we can see on a daily basis.

In previous times of mankind's history people were persecuted for merely speaking of extraordinary experiences. How many people died in the past five hundred or a thousand years - burned at the stake or hung - for having special insights or talents? Has it been this very fear of retribution handed down through generations that has kept many of us silent? Are we still afraid? What will it take for us to trust our own instincts? After all, are we not sharing this rock with other species while hurtling through space?

How much more depth and meaning would our lives contain if we took a deeper look or listened a little closer to Life in all its forms? What might happen if we paid more attention to our pets or the plants around us? How much richer would our experiences become if we embraced the deaths of our loved ones instead of fearing that our turn is coming?

You are a unique individual being whether you see yourself as a citizen of a certain country, a member of a church, a physical body, a set of emotions, a mind, a subconscious, spirit or soul. There is no one else like you.

No matter what you believe or accept as reality, you are still you. Who and what you are, is for you to learn. Are you listening to the clues right in front of you? Have we arrived in this life only to gather things or to merely survive? Where did we actually come from in the first place? What are we doing here and what are our individual purposes for being here? It all boils down to the same question: Who are we, really?

About The Author

Born on Miami Beach in the middle of a hurricane, Robert Munster's life has been a whirlwind from the get-go. Moving from Florida with his family of five siblings, he spent his formative years in Maine. After being drafted and spending a year in Vietnam, Robert has lived a nomadic lifestyle in response to inner guidance. Having resided in Massachusetts, Michigan, California, Oregon, Nevada, Montana, Utah, and Hawaii, he continues that trend by splitting his time between the Dominican Republic and Maine.

Mr. Munster has spent thirty five years as an Occupational Therapist working in numerous medically related settings including acute and long term rehabilitation, home health, schools and private practice. He continues to participate in multi-hands therapy programs utilizing inter-species communication and behavior to promote the healing process.

During the summers Robert Munster lives in his sixteen-sided, two-story home in the middle of the Maine woods. Not far from the Atlantic, Robert loves to spend time in his gardens growing vegetables, fruits, flowers and medicinal herbs.

When not gardening, writing, editing or involved in building projects, you will find him engaged in varied, outdoor activities.

These include kayaking, surfing, biking, picking wild fruit or hunting edible mushrooms in the mountains and forests.

When not surfing or writing, Robert spends the winter months involved in sustainable agriculture and creating educational programs. In between and around his many projects, he always finds the time for a trip to snow covered mountains or a new country. In alignment with his lifestyle, Robert is presently an editor and travel writer for *The Vacation Rental Travel Guide*.

Robert lives with his sweetheart and regularly visits his children and grandchildren who reside in California. Nicknamed Duay, Robert spends as many hours as possible hanging out with the kids doing whatever comes up. Sending the parents away for a night or a weekend, Duay and the crew can be found partying up a storm, watching a show and eating ice cream or popcorn until the wee hours of 8:30p.m.

Other Inspired Living Books

www.DaretoDetoxify.com   www.SuzanneLandry.com   www.TheFreshFoodChef.com

www.TheNewestSecret.com   www.TheRippleEffectGame.com

www.ingramcontent.com/pod-product-compliance
Lightning Source LLC
Chambersburg PA
CBHW060016050426
42448CB00012B/2783